JANE ADDAMS

Jane Addams as she looked when she established Hull-House in 1889.

MAKERS OF AMERICA

JANE ADDAMS

JANE HOVDE

Facts On File
New York • Oxford

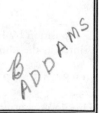

Jane Addams

Copyright © 1989 by Jane Hovde

Facts On File
460 Park Avenue South
New York, New York 10016

Library of Congress Cataloging-in-Publication Data

Hovde, Jane.
    Jane Addams.

    (Makers of America)
    Includes index.
    Bibliography: p.
    1. Addams, Jane, 1860–1935. 2. Social workers—United
States—Biography. 3. Women social workers—United
States—Biography. I. Title. II. Series: Makers of
America (Facts On File, Inc.)
HV28.A35H68   1989   361'.92'4 [B]   88-31051
ISBN 0-8160-1547-3

British CIP data available on request

Facts On File books are available at special
discounts when purchased in bulk quantities
for businesses, associations, institutions,
or sales promotion. Please contact the Special
Sales Department at 212/683-2244.
(Dial 1-800-322-8755, except in NY, AK, HI)

Composition by Facts On File, Inc.
Printed in the United States

10 9 8 7 6 5 4 3 2 1

CONTENTS

CREDITS
Photographs of Jane Addams: (pp. 130) Jane Addams Papers, Swarthmore College Peace Collection; (pp. 137) National Archives. All other photographs are from the Jane Addams Memorial Collection, Special Collections, the University Library, University of Illinois at Chicago. I am indebted to Ronald Beam of Cedarville for the original print of the John Addams's Mills at Cedarville (pp. 21), which was photographed by Dianne Arndt.

1

"ONWARD CHRISTIAN SOLDIERS"—Chicago, 1912

The sky was overcast and the temperature moderate for August as the final and unusual events in the formation of a new political party unfolded at the Chicago Coliseum. With its huge barrel roof and the pseudo-medieval battlements and towers that made up its facade, the Coliseum was in many ways representative of the city. It was an ugly building, but its sheer size made it attractive to large political conventions. It had been used by the Republican Party in both 1908 and 1912, and now on August 7, 1912, it was the site of the new National Progressive Party's convention, which seemed to many a culmination of the great movement for reform that had captured the imagination and energy of many Americans during the first decade of the twentieth century.

It was fitting that the National Progressive Party Convention, which embodied the hope of so many reformers, should have been held in Chicago—a city created by the industrial and urban revolution that had so rapidly transformed America in the latter part of the nineteenth century. With its enormous wealth gaudily displayed in opulent mansions, and its sprawling working-class districts where the poor lived in unsanitary and overcrowded shacks and tenements, Chicago was the prototype of the "new" city of the industrial age. Chicago was the railroad center of America; it was the meat-packers' empire; it was a leading manufacturing center. But above all, it was a city devoted to making money and not to making life liveable and decent for the mass of its citizenry. As the horrors of this industrial colossus became more apparent, a vigorous labor movement and a group of middle-class reformers directed attention to Chicago's problems, slowly changing public thinking about the way the city should be run.

In 1903, Lincoln Steffens, a journalist who used his pen to expose the evils of the new industrial society, said that Chicago was "first in violence, deepest in dirt; loud, lawless, unlovely, ill-smelling, irreverent, new; an overgrown gawk of a village, the 'tough' among cities, a spectacle for the nation. . . ." It displayed marvels of ingenuity, like setting high buildings "on rafts floating in mud." But it wasn't clever enough to "solve the smoke nuisance," or "quench the stench of the stockyards."

Steffens also recognized the meaning of the reform movement in Chicago. "Politically and morally speaking," he said, "Chicago should be celebrated among American cities for reform, real reform, . . . reform that reforms, slow, sure, political, democratic reform, ..."

Chicago, Steffens concluded, "has something to teach every city and town in the country." Now, in 1912, many Chicago reformers were part of an unusual convention. They were there to take what they had learned in Chicago to the nation as a whole.

At 2:22 P.M. the event for which all had been waiting occurred: Theodore Roosevelt's name was placed in nomination for president. Now the former Republican Senator Albert Beveridge, chairman of the convention, pounded the gavel to restore order before introducing the woman who would second the party's nomination on behalf of all American women and the delegates dedicated to the reform platform. Handsome, flawlessly dressed and eloquent, he had already in his keynote address fired the passions of the vast crowd in the coliseum, calling for a national policy of "social brotherhood as against savage individualism" and a "nobler America." An avid expansionist in the debate over the annexation of the Philippines in 1899, Beveridge became more progressive in his demand for social reform legislation with each passing year. His most eloquent moment in the Senate came with his speech in opposition to child labor—the cause for which the woman he now introduced had done so much—Miss Jane Addams, "America's most preeminent and most beloved woman."

Born in 1860, Jane Addams bridged two eras. Her father's life represented the great days of the frontier and the building of the railroads that sped the development of Chicago from a frontier town to an industrial city. Her childhood was filled with echoes of the great debate and the war over slavery, and her ideas of heroism had been formed by the image of her father's political friend—the savior of American democracy in the nineteenth century, Abraham Lincoln.

Addams's mature life was planted firmly in the new industrial age. The rapid emergence of an urban-industrial society, which began in her childhood, had brought in its wake fundamental changes in the conditions of life and the nature of work. It benefited some, but it robbed others of their health (and some of their lives). It also deprived many of a reasonable livelihood or a liveable home.

Jane Addams supported the platforms of the Progressive Party because she embraced the cause of the laborer and his family and espoused the right of women to participate in politics in order to address the evils of modern industrial America.

As Jane Addams rose to address the delegates, she was greeted by a chorus of deafening cheers. Dressed simply in white, the short, motherly, middle-aged lady quietly stood to address the delegates. Her speech was brief and to the point:

> I rise to second the nomination stirred by the splendid platform adopted by this convention. Measures of industrial ameliora-tion, demands for social justice, long discussed by small

groups in charity conferences and economic associations, have
here been considered in a great national convention and are at
last thrust into the stern arena of political action.

It was "inevitable," she continued, that the Progressive Party
should appeal to women, with its program of human welfare.
The Progressive Party properly sought "to draw upon the
great reservoir of their moral energy so long undesired and
unutilized in practical politics." The program holds out the
promise, she said, "that no class of evils shall lie beyond
redress."

As Jane Addams stepped down from the platform, she was
greeted by cheering and the waving of flags and red
bandannas, the symbol of the convention. Women carrying a
yellow banner bearing the words "Votes For Women" stepped
behind her as she walked to her seat, beginning an impromptu
parade. The whole convention burst out singing, "Mine eyes
have seen the glory of the coming of the Lord," and as the
procession proceeded around the hall, even hardened old
politicians seemed "to turn all of a sudden into religious
devotees and whirling dervishes." Delegates shouted, "Pass
prosperity around," and the demonstration ended with the
singing of "Onward Christian Soldiers."

Although there were other nominating speeches for
Roosevelt, the newspapers focused on Jane Addams's. The
Chicago Tribune stated that her appearance in making the
seconding address in a national convention was a marker in
the political history of the nation. An editorial in the
Philadelphia North American stated that her address was "one of
the greatest examples of pure oratory since Lincoln's address
at Gettysburg." It continued enthusiastically, "When Jane
Addams, the foremost citizen of Illinois, rose in the Progressive Convention and seconded the nomination of
Theodore Roosevelt for President, it marked an important
step forward in the cause of social and industrial justice. She is
one of the ten greatest citizens of this republic."

In reporting the events of the Progressive Convention,
newspapers commented on the unusual nature of this political
meeting. Some described it as a great moral movement, not-

Roosevelt and Addams, 1912, Boston Journal.

ing the enthusiasm, earnestness, and sincerity of the assemblage of so many well-known reformers and social workers. Jane Addams described it this way:

> Suddenly, as if by magic, the city of Chicago, became filled with men and women from every state in the Union who were evidently haunted by the same social compunctions and animated by like hopes. . . . [I]t did not seem in the least strange

that reticent men and women should speak aloud their religious and social beliefs, confident that they would be understood.

Not the least of the unusual features of the convention was the number of women who attended and took part as delegates. Although women had made their first official appearance at the National Republican Convention in 1892, their numbers at conventions had been miniscule and their presence little felt. At this convention women were represented by a dozen women delegates whose impact was greater than their numbers.

The unusual makeup of the convention derived from the origins of this new party. The party's formation arose out of the union of the movement for social justice that had been growing since the end of the nineteenth century and the interests of a dynamic and charismatic political leader—Theodore Roosevelt—who had dominated American politics since becoming president in 1901.

As the youngest and most vigorous man ever to serve in the White House, Theodore Roosevelt had an enormous impact on the American people. To Americans who loved him, he was the hero of the Rough Riders at San Juan Hill and a constant battler for right. Although only 5 feet 8 inches in height, he seemed massive, his muscular frame weighing two hundred pounds. In 1912 he was a bit slower in movement, a bit heavier around the waist. He was becoming gray around the temples, but with his celebrated toothy grin he had lost none of his old power to evoke an enthusiastic response from the crowds.

A skilled politician, Roosevelt had made the presidency a powerful office, and he used his power boldly. He saw the president as a "steward of the people bound actively and affirmatively to do all he could for the people." As president, he had given effective expression to the program of reforms that social workers, civic reformers, and progressive politicians were demanding to change the economic and political character of the country. To be sure, except for a few positive acts, he had aided the cause of reform more in the response he invoked. In speeches and addresses he had aroused the nation to the need for action.

Although a third term would have been his for the asking, and he really enjoyed being president and loved the power the office brought him, Roosevelt decided not to run again in 1908 and had passed the mantle of leadership of the Republican Party and the presidency on to William Howard Taft. Already the Republican Party had begun to divide between conservatives and a group of middle western progressive Republicans, including Wisconsin's Senator Robert La Follette, who were pressing for economic, social, and political reforms. This split continued to widen as President Taft moved toward the conservative wing of the party and in 1910 broke with the progressive Republicans.

Roosevelt returned to the United States in 1910 from his extended vacation in Europe and Africa to find the Republican Party in shambles. Personally estranged from Taft, he went on a speaking tour to defend progressive Republican principles. At Osawatomie, Kansas, he celebrated the memory of John Brown with a speech in which he supported advanced social legislation by the federal government. Roosevelt criticized judges who ruled that it was not lawful under the Constitution for governments to limit or control some of the evil practices of business. There was a fervor of response to Roosevelt, and it was only a matter of time before he would be convinced that he should "throw his hat into the ring"—that only he could win for the Republicans in 1912.

The pre-convention campaign established beyond a doubt the popular demand for Roosevelt's nomination as the Republican candidate for president. But President Taft and the conservatives of the party had no thought of permitting that, and they were in firm control of the party organization at the Republican Convention and the credentials committee that decided contested delegates. Defeated at the Republican Party Convention in June, Roosevelt's supporters decided to bolt the party and hold a "rump" convention to nominate Roosevelt. Later they determined that a real convention should be called to establish a new third party with a platform of principles. Thus Roosevelt returned to Chicago in August 1912 to be nominated as the presidential candidate of the National Progressive Party.

Roosevelt's strategy for the new party was clear. He sensed the country wanted a reformer in the White House, so he determined that his new party would address the political, social, and industrial issues that had concerned reformers for more than a decade. With few professional Republican politicians in his camp, he embraced the reformers, taking the "social standards of industry," as the social workers called their minimum platform, as the basis of the social and industrial planks of the Progressive Party platform.

These minimum standards had been drafted by a committee of the National Conference of Charities, which had been appointed in 1909, the year Jane Addams was elected as its first woman president. They represented the common platform for the agitations conducted separately by such groups as the National Child Labor Committee, the National Consumer's League, the Woman's Trade Union League, the American Association for Labor Legislation, and the National Tuberculosis Association.

These organizations were concerned with defining minimum social and industrial standards necessary for any "community interested in self-preservation." They included proposals for minimum-wage boards, a living minimum wage, an eight-hour day, a six-day week, safety and health regulations, the right to a home, the prohibition of child labor under sixteen, abolition of sweatshops, and social insurance against sickness, unemployment, industrial accidents, and old age. A group of social workers had gone to the Republican Convention to present this minimum platform of social standards, but the Republicans were not interested. Paul Kellogg, the chairman of the Committee on Industrial Standards, wrote to Jane Addams that he had had a session with Roosevelt at Oyster Bay, New York, in July after Roosevelt's defeat at the Republican Convention. The committee's "report was all grist to T.R.'s mill in launching the Progressive Party during that summer . . . and he took over the Cleveland program of standards of life and labor practically bodily, and it was, as you know, incorporated in the Progressive platform."

Jane Addams did indeed know that the report had been incorporated into the Progressive platform. She had been asked to join Roosevelt's party and was an important member of the party's platform committee. In the face of criticism that partisan politics was not a proper role for women, Addams had entered politics in 1912 because the new party stood for "social hopes so long ignored by the politicians." It was not just the Progressives' stand for social justice, however, it was also their support of woman suffrage that influenced her decision. For a number of years Addams had worked for woman suffrage as a necessary instrument to the realization of many of the reforms she supported. Matters formerly private and of particular concern to women, such as the disposal of garbage and the health of children, had become public issues, but had been slighted by American political institutions. The political participation of women, Addams felt, was essential to a better urban and industrial environment.

Jane Addams knew that Roosevelt stood for woman suffrage because she had listened to him—some say influenced him to—endorse equal suffrage publicly for the first time in 1911. He assured her in August 1912 that he was "without qualification or equivocation" for woman suffrage. According to Hull-House accounts, Roosevelt had visited Jane Addams in Chicago in March 1911 and had ridden with her to a large public meeting at the Chicago Armory to honor a group of immigrants who had just become naturalized citizens. On the way to the meeting Roosevelt and Addams discussed votes for women, and after a very persuasive presentation by Jane Addams, Roosevelt admitted that there were good arguments for it, adding that "of course, you are one of the best arguments yourself." Much to Addams's surprise, Roosevelt declared in his address to the immigrants that, for the best interests of the country, he had always believed that women, like naturalized male aliens, should have the vote.

The issue of woman suffrage was of growing concern and urgency to Jane Addams in the summer of 1912. The woman suffrage movement had begun as early as 1848 at a Woman's

Rights Convention in Seneca Falls, New York, where the first American suffragists, such as Elizabeth Cady Stanton, had called for equal rights for women, including the vote. With the beginning of the twentieth century the movement had become united and strong; women had achieved the vote in some states, but they had become impatient with the slow state-by-state approach. As vice-president of the National American Woman Suffrage Association, Addams had earlier in the year led a group to Washington to testify in favor of a federal suffrage amendment, just as women had done for forty-two consecutive sessions of Congress. The House Judiciary Committee, as it had done so many times before, agreed only to take the petition of the women "under advisement."

By 1912 Jane Addams believed that the various reforms, including woman suffrage, which had been adopted in certain cities and states needed to be extended nationally. She believed that the American people were ready to endorse them. Now she and her fellow reform advocates were being given an opportunity through the Progressive platform to take their program to the country. 1912 was the year of her greatest hopes, and she was the woman who could bring those hopes to fulfillment.

At fifty-two she was no longer the frail-looking young woman who had arrived in Chicago in 1889 with a new idea that quickly spread—the neighborhood settlement. The settlement concept—living in a poor and needy neighborhood of a city, knowing the residents and their problems, and providing help—had originated with Toynbee Hall. Jane Addams had visited Toynbee Hall, which had been established for graduates of Oxford and Cambridge Universities in one of the poorest districts of London in 1884. She thought such an establishment in her own country would offer a way for college-educated young men and women in comfortable circumstances "to give tangible expression to the democratic ideal" and to serve in an "experimental effort to aid in the solution of the social and individual problems which are engendered by the modern conditions of life in a great city."

This idea led Jane Addams and her friend, Ellen Starr, to move into a dilapidated mansion, soon to be called Hull-House, which was located in the Nineteenth Ward, one of Chicago's poorest and most overcrowded working-class districts. They invited their immigrant neighbors to evenings of readings, music, and a viewing of art photographs that they had brought back from Europe. They also began classes and clubs. People soon came to them with their troubles, like the peasant German woman whose "four years in America had been spent in patiently carrying water up and down two flights of stairs and in washing the heavy flannel suits of iron foundry workers . . . for thirty-five cents a day." And the women learned about the conditions of the working families of Chicago simply by making Hull-House a social center. "Our very first Christmas at Hull-House," Jane Addams wrote:

> when we as yet knew nothing of child labor, a number of little girls refused candy which was offered them as part of the Christmas good cheer saying simply that they "worked in a candy factory and could not bear the sight of it." We discovered for six weeks they had worked from seven in the morning until nine at night, and they were exhausted as well as satiated. The sharp consciousness of stern economic conditions was thrust upon us in the midst of the season of good will.

In the beginning Hull-House activities were almost entirely social and educational, but not for long. "At first Hull-House was largely committed to education, which is the traditional American approach to every problem," Jane Addams later stated, "but from the very beginning I am happy to say the educational process was mutual." The Hull-House women became educated in the problems of their neighborhood and began to define a new social and public role for women. Jane Addams probably would have smiled in disbelief if anyone had told her in 1889 that the logic of what she was doing would inevitably bring her into politics. But obtaining clean milk for babies meant entering politics, even national politics.

Addams explained why this was so. "For years," she said, "an effort has been made in Chicago to obtain clean milk,

upon which the health of city children so absolutely depends."
For years, however, clean milk had been almost impossible to
obtain because the supply came from thousands of tubercular
cows in the nearby states. "Clean milk," she said, "demands
an inspection of the dairy farms of Wisconsin, Michigan, Indiana and Iowa, as well as Illinois."

It soon became clear to the women at Hull-House that the
urban problems they faced were too much for philanthropy
and individual effort; politics became central to their activity.
They made careful investigations, exposed social problems,
and lobbied legislators for laws to curtail the exploitation of
workers, limit child labor, shorten working hours for
women, and arbitrate labor disputes. Hull-House was the
seedbed for many of the ideas embodied in the Progressive
platform, and it was the political activity of the Hull-House
women that helped to bring these issues to public attention.
Now with the prospect of woman suffrage nearer, there
seemed no limit to the reforms that might be achieved with
the participation of all women in political life.

Letters from Addams's friends and fellow social workers
were enthusiastic in response to the events of the convention.
"How great you were to carry off a political party at the
strategic moment," wrote Mary McDowell of the University
of Chicago Settlement. "Aren't you magnificent?" Katherine
Coman, a Wellesley economics professor wrote. "What a
grand new service you have rendered the human race!
Thousands of women are blessing you this day because your
new leadership brings us perceptively nearer to the Kingdom
of Heaven."

Three years later a political analyst wrote:

> The most significant incident connected with Roosevelt's
> nomination was the seconding speech made by Jane Addams of
> Chicago. This speech was the entrance of women into national
> politics in a new sense, and, in addition to giving tremendous
> impetus to the suffrage movement, drew to the Progressive
> party the support of thousands of women in those states where
> women have the right to vote.

The enthusiasm of 1912 and the analysis of 1915 were premature. It was true that women got the vote in 1919 and that some of the reforms the women at Hull-House had sought were enacted into law in the 1920's. But the expectations of Jane Addams that woman suffrage would hasten reform were not realized. Women as a group did not become the agents of reform, and the reform movement itself was a victim of the long war in Europe. By 1915 Jane Addams had turned to international politics and diplomacy in an attempt to bring about peace, knowing full well that there could be no social justice without peace.

The story of Jane Addams and the Hull-House women is central to understanding the development and operation of American democracy and the emergence of women as a prime factor in American politics.

2

CEDARVILLE

Jane Addams's journey to Hull–House in Chicago and the problems of an industrial and urban America led her from one kind of world to another. She was born in 1860 and grew up in the picturesque, wooded village of Cedarville in northwestern Illinois, 12 miles from the Wisconsin state line and about 40 miles from the Mississippi River. Here her father and mother had settled sixteen years earlier.

Illinois was still something of a pioneer state in 1844 when John Addams and his bride, Sarah, made their ten-day trip from Pennsylvania by way of New York City and Niagara Falls to Chicago, just eleven days after their marriage. Although Illinois had been a state since 1818, its northern sections remained largely uninhabited except by Indians who, in a 1804 treaty with the government, had given up their lands but were not required to leave until the line of settlement reached them. In the 1820's federal government agents asked them to move. The Indians did leave; however, a dissident group, led by an old war chief, Black Hawk, denied the validity of the treaty and returned to its Rock River village in

1831. As a result, whites waged a war of extermination against the Indians, called the Black Hawk War.

With the Indians out of the way, settlers began to pour into the area, attracted by the fertile prairie land of northwest Illinois. John and Sarah Addams were among those who came. With the building of canals and roads linking the East to the Midwest, and the rising demand for food from eastern commercial cities and factory towns, prospects for the area looked good.

Jane Addams always maintained that her father was the dominant influence on her life. Little is known about him before his emigration to Illinois. Of English ancestry, he was born in Pennsylvania in 1822, the seventh of ten children. His grandfather served as a captain in the Revolutionary War, but had died before John was born. As a young man, John, after a brief experience teaching school, had become a miller's apprentice at Ambler near Philadelphia. In his leisure time he "read all the books in the village library" and developed an interest in history. The following entry in his diary suggests the commitment to integrity for which he later became well-known: "Am firmly impressed that 'Honesty is the best Policy' and hope that I may by all means and through all hazards stick to the above Proverb." John Addams served four years as a miller's apprentice and acquired the flattened "miller's thumb" that comes from feeling the flour between the thumb and forefinger to determine its quality. At the age of twenty-two he married his employer's sister-in-law, Sarah Weber.

Sarah, five years older than John Addams, was the daughter of George Weber, a prosperous and established miller who owned land and a flour mill near Kreidersville, Pennsylvania. For some time before the wedding, there had been a family discussion about "going west." Relatives of Sarah's family had already settled near Freeport in Illinois, and Sarah's father was of the opinion that a mill in that area would be extremely profitable. Finally the family decided that not only John and Sarah, but also George Weber, should make the trip to Illinois.

The trip is recorded in John Addams's diary. He wrote on the morning of July 29, 1844, "Myself and Wife left Kreidersville at four A.M. in a two-wheeled conveyance," first for Somerville, New Jersey, and then "by Railroad" and "arrived at the Great City of New York at 11 o'clock P.M., travelling 47 Miles in three hours." Accompanied by Sarah's father, they continued their journey to Albany on the *Knickerbocker*. It was a "splendid boat," as John wrote, "with pleasant state-room." From Albany they took a train to Buffalo, a city "destined in my humble opinion to become one of the most Noted Places along the Lakes." Since this was their honeymoon, they went the next day to Niagara Falls. That afternoon, they boarded the *St. Louis*, a fine steamer on her first trip to Chicago, and arrived at the city on August 8.

Chicago did not favorably impress John Addams. He noted that the town "was commenced ten years ago and now has a population of about 8 thousand—nearly every person is engaged in some mercantile business, in my opinion too many for the place." He also commented that the business district was "Located entirely too Low."

In 1848, just four years after the Addams's brief visit, John L. Peyton in *Over the Alleghenies* gave a more detailed account of the rapidly growing city. Already twenty thousand people were settled on the level piece of ground "half dry and half wet, resembling a salt marsh" on both sides of the Chicago River, "a sluggish slimy stream, too lazy to clean itself." Manufacturing was becoming important. "Large establishments," Peyton wrote:

> were engaged in manufacturing agricultural implements of every description for the farmers who flocked to the country every spring. A single establishment, that of McCormick, employed several hundred hands, and during each season completed from fifteen hundred to two thousand grain-reapers and grass-mowers. Blacksmith, wagon and coachmaker's shops were busy preparing for the spring demand, which with all their energy they could not supply.

The problems of rapid growth and a lack of concern about living conditions were already evident in 1848. "There was no pavement," Peyton wrote:

> no macadamized streets, no drainage, and the three thousand
> houses in which the people lived, were almost entirely small
> timber buildings . . . defaced by mud. . . . To render the streets
> and sidewalks passable they were covered with boards. . . .
> Under these planks the water was standing on the surface . . .
> and the sewers from the houses were emptied under them, a
> frightful odor was emitted in summer, causing fevers and other
> diseases.

John Addams did not stay long in Chicago. His future prosperity would be linked with the city, but its clamor and frenzy were not for him. His diary indicates that the day after he arrived in Chicago he decided to leave.

After three months of exploring northern Illinois, John Addams purchased from two pioneer settlers a sawmill and gristmill—the first mill in Stephenson County, erected six years earlier. He also purchased eighty acres of woodland adjoining it on the Cedar Creek six miles north of Freeport, and it was there he settled.

Jane Addams later described the Cedar Creek area. "The prairie," she wrote:

> was broken into hills, one of them crowned by pine woods,
> grown up from a bag full of Norway pine seeds sown by my
> father in 1844, the very year he came to Illinois. . . . The banks
> of the mill stream rose into high bluffs too perpendicular to be
> climbed without skill, and containing caves of which one at
> least was so black that it could not be explored without the aid
> of a candle.

In 1844 there was no village of Cedarville. Active settlement began the year John and Sarah arrived. Prospects looked promising to John Addams. The good agricultural and forest land provided grain and lumber for his mills; the problem was access to markets for his products.

John Addams put his faith in the railroad; he was a leading figure in a convention held at Rockford to organize the building of the Chicago and Galena line. This railroad would link the farming communities of northwestern Illinois, not only to Chicago and to markets in the East, but also to the Mississippi River at Galena, and from there to markets in the South.

This somewhat imaginative drawing of the Addams mills at Cedarville, made in 1871, shows the development of rural industry in northwestern Illinois with the building of the Chicago and Galena Railroad.

Funds for this purpose had to be raised by persuading the farmers of the importance of the railroad and getting them to purchase stock in the company. Most of the stock was sold in small amounts, one or two shares. John Addams, not yet twenty-four, undertook the job of securing subscriptions in Stephenson County. By 1848 enough money had been raised to begin construction. While only $20,000 was raised in Chicago, Addams had raised more than $20,000 in Stephenson County. Although it was ten years before the railroad reached Freeport, it was profitable from the start.

Through his efforts in behalf of the railroad, John Addams became the best-known man in the district. In 1854, when the Republican Party was organized, he ran as the Republican candidate for the state senate from his county and served in this position continuously until 1870, achieving a statewide reputation for honesty. He later refused a nomination to be governor and repeatedly declined to run for the U.S. Congress. In 1858 he built one of the largest and best-equipped mills in the area, grinding one hundred barrels of flour daily, which were then shipped west to Galena on the Mississippi and east to Chicago. Addams was one of the first to profit handsomely from the building of the Chicago and Galena Railroad, both from his investment in the line and greater profits from his mill. He also purchased more land and invested in other Illinois railroads. During the Civil War he helped to organize the Second National Bank of Freeport and served as its president until his death in 1881. His estate, mostly in land, was valued at $350,000, a fortune for that section of Illinois at that time.

With access to the railroad, the village of Cedarville grew. In 1850 James Canfield set up a brick kiln; soon there was a brick store and the Addams family had a new brick house. A tin shop, three blacksmiths' shops, and a tavern became part of the town's economy. Small factories, which later became important, were started. The Henney Carriage Works was the largest carriage factory in the West and exported its vehicles to Europe, Australia, and South America. By 1854 the population of the village had reached four hundred; in 1871 it reached its peak of seven hundred.

John Addams was a community leader as well as a business leader, and he played an important role in developing the town's cultural and educational institutions. In 1846 he helped campaign for funds for the first public school. He also started the first subscription library, which was initially housed in the Addams's home. He was influential in organizing at least two of the four churches in town, and he conducted classes at the Union Sunday school for many years.

The chronicle of John Addams's life in Illinois is much like the proverbial American success story. And from the bare outline known of the life of Sarah Addams, a typical picture emerges of the women who accompanied the men West. In the earlier days in Cedarville the family home was the center of John Addams's milling and agricultural enterprises. With always two or three hired girls to help, Sarah Addams ran what amounted to a domestic factory, doing much of the work herself. Until the arrival of the railroad, Cedarville was cut off from major urban centers, and therefore, the household produced its own soap, lard, candles, rugs, quilts, and stockings, as well as preserving meat, canning fruits and vegetables, and baking bread. Mrs. Addams prepared meals daily for as many as twenty farm and mill hands, in addition to the family. She also knew the mill business and took charge when her husband was away at the state legislature or on business trips.

Women like Sarah Addams might have the satisfaction of contributing much to the family income, but the work was not easy, particularly with the birth of a new baby on the average of every two years. Raising a large family in mid-nineteenth-century America was also not without its perils—both to the women and to their children. Like many mothers of the period, Sarah Addams had to face and cope with family tragedy. Of the nine children she bore by the time she was forty-six, only four survived to adulthood. She saw one child die at two months, another at ten months, still another at two years. In January 1863 Sarah Addams, seven months pregnant with her ninth child, was called to help in the wagon-maker's wife's delivery in the absence of the local doctor. While helping her neighbor Sarah collapsed and was carried home, where she gave birth to a stillborn baby girl. She herself died a week later.

Jane Addams was only two when her mother died. John Addams was Jane's only parent for the six years before he married Anna Haldeman in 1869. Her four remaining siblings, Mary, Martha, Weber, and Alice, were all much older than Jane. Mary, the oldest, just seventeen at her mother's death, took over the management of the household and especially the care of her little sister.

Mary was always frail, but in other ways she was said to be much like her mother—thoughtful, affectionate, and competent. After John Addams's remarriage, she left home and attended nearby Rockford Female Seminary for a brief time before marrying the Presbyterian minister of Cedarville.

When she was grown Jane spent considerable time in Mary's home, helping out when Mary was pregnant or ill, or when her family made one of its frequent moves.

Martha, the second oldest and "the beauty of the family," lived just a few years after her mother's death; she died of typhoid fever when Jane was only six. Jane later told her sister Alice that after Martha's death her "horrible dream every night would be Mary's death and no one to love me."

Weber, Jane's only surviving brother, was ten when his mother died and too old to be a companion to Jane in her childhood. He later married and had a farm in Cedarville. After Jane's father died, he took over the operation of the mills. As an adult, Weber suffered from acute depression and was in and out of mental institutions; Jane took care of his family and his affairs when he had a mental breakdown in 1883.

Alice, her closest sister in age, was seven years older than Jane, and she left home to attend Rockford Female Seminary when Jane was nine. Alice, the most vigorous of the Addams children, was both adventurous and strong-willed. She married her stepbrother, Harry Haldeman, despite opposition from her father and stepmother.

Jane's early childhood years must have been somewhat lonely and somber. At an early age she had to learn to deal with illnesses and death, although she did not record any recollection of a direct contact with death until she was fifteen. "Word came to us one Sunday evening," she wrote later:

> that Polly was dying. . . . Polly was an old nurse who had taken care of my mother. . . . I was the only person able to go to her. I left the lamp-lit, warm house to be driven four miles through a blinding storm which every minute added more snow to the already high drifts, with a sense of starting upon a fateful errand.

Upon arrival Jane was left alone with Polly.

> The square, old-fashioned chamber in the lonely farmhouse was very cold and still with nothing to be heard but the storm outside. Suddenly the great change came. . . . [In] place of the

face familiar from my earliest childhood and associated with
homely household chores, there lay upon the pillow strange,
august features, stern and withdrawn from all the small affairs
of life. . . . As I was driven home in the winter storm, the wind
through the trees seemed laden with a passing soul and the
riddle of life and death pressed hard; once to be young, to grow
old and to die, everything came to that. . . .

As a child, Jane had a succession of illnesses, the most
serious of which was, apparently, tuberculosis of the spine.
This left her with a slight curvature of the back, causing her to
carry her head cocked a bit to one side. In the days before
modern drugs, tuberculosis of the lung was a major cause of
death in the United States, outstripping cancer and heart disease. Tuberculosis flourished particularly among the laboring
class in crowded, unsanitary urban slums. Tuberculosis of the
spine, a rarer form of the disease, was more common in
children under five. Although little is known about Jane's experience with this illness, it clearly affected her self-image.
She mentions in her autobiography that she saw herself as an
"ugly pigeon-toed little girl, whose crooked back obliged her
to walk with her head much to one side," and she worried that
"'strange people' should know that my handsome father
owned this homely little girl."

Writing about her memories of childhood many years later
in *Twenty Years at Hull-House*, Jane Addams depicted herself as
an introspective and somber little girl seeking approval from a
serious-minded father upon whom she centered all of her
affection. She described her father as "dignified" and
"handsome." Seeing him at church, where he taught a Bible
class to the Union Sunday School, she wrote, "to my eyes at
least [he] was a most imposing figure in his Sunday frock coat,
his fine head rising high above all the others." To his con-
temporaries John Addams seemed reserved. Jane referred to
him as "grave."

Jane Addams adored her father and sought to model herself
in his image. As she wrote: "Doubtless I centered upon him all
the careful imitation which a little girl ordinarily gives to her
mother's way and habits. . . . I had a consuming ambition to

possess a miller's thumb," she wrote, "and would sit contentedly for a long time rubbing between my thumb and fingers the ground wheat as it fell from between the millstones." She resolved to read all the books in his library just as he, as a young miller's apprentice, had read all the books in the village library. John Addams encouraged her in her intellectual development, rewarding her for every life she read in Plutarch's *Lives* and for every volume of such books as Irving's *Life of Washington*.

It was her father, Jane said, who also first drew her "into the moral concerns of life." She recalled the "horrid nights when I tossed about in my bed because I had told a lie . . . held in the grip of a miserable dread of death, a double fear, first that I should die in my sins . . . and second, that my father—representing the entire adult world which I had basely deceived—should himself die before I had time to tell him." The only way to obtain relief was to go downstairs, conquering all fear of the night, to confess her sin. She always received the same assurance "that if he 'had a little girl who told lies,' he was very glad that she 'felt too bad to go to sleep afterwards.'" "No absolution was asked for nor received," she reported, "but apparently the sense that the knowledge of my wickedness was shared, or an obscure understanding of the affection which underlay the grave statement, was sufficient, for I always went back to bed as bold as a lion and slept, if not the sleep of the just, at least that of the comforted."

On the many occasions that she confided her sins and perplexities to her father, she remembered few times when she received direct advice. Yet he clearly communicated to her the message that she ought to prize "mental integrity above everything else." John Addams was not a religious man in the sense of professing a specific religious creed, although he attended one or another of the churches in Cedarville. For her father, as for many other Americans of the mid-nineteenth century, religion was an ideal of personal conduct; an insistence on self-reliance and total honesty.

Jane's one remembrance of anything like a scolding from her father was when, at the age of eight, she wanted him to tell her how fine she looked in her new cloak. She was upset by his remark that it was "a very pretty cloak—in fact so much prettier than any cloak the other little girls in the Sunday School had." Wear your old cloak, he advised his daughter. It would keep her quite warm, "with the added advantage of not making the other little girls feel badly." It was "very stupid," John said, to wear expensive clothes that set up barriers between you and others in a world where all should strive to live as equals.

Shortly after her father's death Jane wrote that he had been respected for his honesty, "an uncompromising enemy of wrong and of wrongdoing. He was . . . a fearless advocate of right things in public life . . . a man of purest and sternest integrity. . . ." She followed her father's model in choosing a life of dedicated public service; trying to live by his high standards, and striving always for moral and intellectual excellence.

In her autobiography, Jane emphasized her father's influence and wrote nothing about her stepmother. However, John Addams's remarriage to Anna Haldeman when Jane was eight marked an important event in Jane's life.

Anna Haldeman was quite different from the first Mrs. Addams. An attractive, high-spirited woman, she was the widow of William Haldeman, a miller in the somewhat larger nearby town of Freeport. Anna Haldeman considered herself an aristocrat and a cultured lady. Although she had little formal education, she grew up in an educated family—both of her brothers had become doctors—and she was an avid reader and an accomplished musician. She equipped the Addams's simple home with furnishings suitable to what she considered was her husband's position. Though she directed and managed the house, she herself did no household work. Fond of society, she entertained her friends and her husband's business and political associates in an elegant way.

The values and life-style of her stepmother influenced Jane Addams. The atmosphere of her stepmother's home probably helped Jane to acquire her social ease. As an adult, she was always seen as a gracious hostess. And although she later rejected the role of the leisured, cultivated lady that her stepmother represented, Jane Addams for some years after college pursued the life of culture that Anna had emphasized in the Addams's home.

While the sophisticated environment of her stepmother's home was one side of Jane's new life, her enjoyment of rural pleasures with her stepbrother George was another. George, one of Anna's sons by her previous marriage, was an intelligent, imaginative boy six months younger than Jane. A keen observer of nature, George encouraged her interest in science; later he himself would do advanced work in biology at Johns Hopkins.

Together George and Jane roamed the countryside, with its cliffs, caves, woods, and streams. They played games "which lasted week after week as only free-ranging country children can do." Jane, in her work at Hull-House, was to show a deep love for urban youth and a deep understanding of their plight. The childhood adventures with George influenced her later analysis of the difficulties confronting young people as they grew up in city slums. "It may be," she wrote later, "that one of the most piteous aspects in the life of city children . . . is the constant interruption to their play which is inevitable on the streets, so that it can never have any continuity." City children lived on the streets; their lives were endlessly disrupted by the passing traffic. They were obliged to begin their games over and over again. "Even the most vivacious," Addams noted, "become worn out at last, and take to that passive 'standing around,' . . . which in time becomes so characteristic of city children."

Growing up during the 1860's, Jane observed the heroism that was played out beyond her village. Her father was a friend of Abraham Lincoln and a faithful supporter of the war that freed the slaves. He raised and equipped a company of soldiers from the Cedarville region.

Cedarville's sons lost their lives in the conflict; the Addams children heard many stories about it. Jane remembered that they enjoyed visiting and talking to an old lady who lived in a white farmhouse north of the village. She was the mother of the village hero, Tommy, and "used to tell us," wrote Jane, "of her long anxiety during the spring of 1862; how she waited day after day for the hospital to surrender up her son. . . ."

Tommy came home at last, in the late spring; but it was clear that he would soon die. "His mother's heart was broken," Jane wrote, "to see him so wan and changed. She would tell us of the long quiet days that followed his return, with the windows open that the dying eyes might look over the orchard slope to the meadow beyond, where the younger brothers were mowing the early hay."

Jane Addams was four and a half when Abraham Lincoln died. She remembered the event vividly. For the first time she saw her father in tears. She grew up not only under her father's spell, but also under Lincoln's, too.

Her admiration for the wartime president was linked with a visit made to see an eagle, "Old Abe," who was housed in the state capitol building of Wisconsin, only sixty-five miles from Cedarville. Old Abe had been the Eighth Wisconsin Regiment's mascot throughout the war. As she "stood under the great white dome of Old Abe's stately home," Jane remembered, she was "filled with the tumultuous impression of soldiers marching to death for freedom's sake. But through all my vivid sensations there persisted the image of the eagle in the corridor below and Lincoln himself as an epitome of all that was great and good."

Thousands of children, like Jane Addams, growing up during the sixties and seventies of the last century, "caught a notion of imperishable heroism when they were told that brave men had lost their lives that the slaves might be free." The new age into which Addams was born needed a new heroism to free men, women, and children from endless, deadly toil. In the course of time she herself would come to symbolize the social conscience of this new age.

3

THE EDUCATION OF JANE ADDAMS

At the age of seventeen Jane Addams was ready to leave Cedarville to attend college at Rockford, Illinois. She was a slender and attractive young woman—five feet three inches tall and ninety-five pounds in weight. She wore her soft, brown hair pulled back and gathered into a bun with a simplicity that emphasized her dark eyes.

Before the Civil War there were few institutions of higher education that women could attend, and most of the existing ones, like the coeducational Oberlin College, did not provide the same quality of education for women as they did for men. Women students at Oberlin followed the "ladies course" and received special degrees. After the Civil War new, endowed colleges for women, modeled on elite eastern male colleges, raised the expectations of young women. Vassar, founded in 1861, Smith in 1872, Wellesley in 1875, and Bryn Mawr in 1886, were engaged in what was then seen as an exciting new experiment to prove that women could undertake a course of study as demanding as that offered in the best men's institutions.

Jane Addams, aware of these new developments, was determined to go to Smith. But her father had other plans. John Addams was a trustee of Rockford Female Seminary and, in accordance with his educational plan, Jane, like her older sisters, was to go to nearby Rockford "to be followed by travel abroad in lieu of the wider advantages which an Eastern school [was] supposed to afford." Jane was, at first, disappointed to be going to Rockford, but agreed to attend for one year, with the hope of entering Smith afterwards. She began at Rockford in 1877 and went on, as it turned out, to complete a full collegiate course of study there. She was one of the first women to be offered a bachelor of arts degree, which she received in 1882.

Rockford Female Seminary, as Addams described it, was "one of the earliest efforts for women's higher education in the Mississippi Valley, and from the beginning was called the Mount Holyoke of the West."

Mount Holyoke in South Hadley, Massachusetts, was founded in 1837 by Mary Lyon as the first endowed residential institution of higher education for women. Its curriculum was advanced for its day, its academic quality high, and its emphasis religious. Rockford inherited, as Addams said, "much of the missionary spirit of [Mount Holyoke], and the proportion of missionaries among its early graduates was almost as large as Mount Holyoke's own." Rockford's first students were keenly aware of the sacrifice their parents had made to send them there; they felt that each minute of the time so dearly bought must be put to good use. This, Addams remembered, "fostered an atmosphere of intensity, a fever of preparation."

Key to this Rockford "atmosphere" was its strong-willed and religious principal, Anna Peck Sill, who ruled over the seminary for thirty-five years. Meticulous in appearance, she exemplified the proper Christian lady in her dresses of subdued color with little white collars of lace or organdy, giving just the right touch of femininity.

Miss Sill's calm appearance barely concealed the intense energy within. She had grown up in western New York when that part of the state was being swept with religious revivals. Anna experienced "conversion"—the recognition and acceptance of the truth of Christ's message—became fired with enthusiasm to devote her life to God's service as a missionary. Having taught in New York State for a number of years, she realized that she could be more useful if she helped bring Christian education "to the wild and more uncultivated prairies of the West."

Miss Sill appeared in Rockford at a time when its citizens and religious leaders wanted to start a seminary for young women. The purpose of the school was "to infuse . . . moral and religious culture, recognizing . . . that character is the end of knowledge, . . . [and] to inspire a missionary spirit." Rockford graduates would be "cultivated Christian women . . . Christian mothers and missionaries."

Many of the seminary graduates indeed became missionaries. Miss Sill tried to win additional converts from each new group of students; Jane Addams, too, was subjected to this pressure. The "unconverted" women like herself, she remembered, "were the subject of prayer at the daily chapel exercises and the weekly prayer meeting, attendance upon which was obligatory."

At the age of eighteen, Ellen Gates Starr arrived at Rockford from the little country town of Durand, Illinois, in 1877. Slight in build and frail in appearance, Ellen had a quick wit; she was a vivacious and intense young lady with a passionate interest in art and nature; she and Jane became friends. They shared confidences and a mutual concern about religion. Responding to a letter from Ellen about the divinity of Christ Jane wrote, "Christ don't help me in the least . . . I didn't pray, at least formally, for about three months, and was shocked to find that I felt no worse for it. . . ."

Religion eventually, for Addams, had little connection with Christian dogma. For her it was a matter of ethics in the service of man.

What exactly her future work would be Jane was not sure. At times she talked of going east to Smith College. She also talked of going to medical school in Edinburgh, Scotland. In any case she was determined to gain a college degree and was a leader in efforts to transform Rockford from a seminary to a degree-granting college. In 1876 the Seminary, reflecting the advances in women's education represented by the newly established eastern women's colleges, instituted a strong collegiate course. However, Miss Sill was not in favor of conferring degrees on young ladies.

Jane Addams and her classmates were "keenly conscious of the growing development of Rockford Seminary into a College" and were enthusiastic about their school's taking its place "in the new movement of full college education for women." Jane's attitude was summed up in a speech given at the junior class exhibition in 1880. She began by noting the recent changes "in the ambition and aspirations of women," changes that could be seen most clearly in women's education. Education for a woman, she said:

> has passed from accomplishments and the arts of pleasing, to the development of [woman's] intellectual force, and her capabilities for direct labor. She wishes not to be a man, nor like a man, but she claims the same right to independent thought and action. . . . [O]n the other hand we still retain the old ideal of womanhood—the Saxon lady whose mission it was to give bread unto her household.

Although the sense of exciting new possibilities ran through the speech, there was a tension between a larger vision of woman's role in the world and the traditional definition of woman as homemaker. Both her father's example and the new attitude toward education for women in the 1870's seemed to offer an opportunity for Jane Addams to challenge the whole doctrine of a woman's "proper sphere." But this would have been an extraordinary leap, given traditional circumstances and attitudes generally and Jane Addams's specific experience at Rockford. She was caught between the call to a life of social usefulness in the world and the traditional convention of woman's domestic role; this caused only confusion and emotional paralysis after she left college.

Meanwhile Jane's years at Rockford contributed to her own growing awareness of her abilities. Her classmates admired her and looked to her for leadership; she excelled in all aspects of college life. She was valedictorian in 1881 and was involved in almost every student activity. Jane relished her studies in Greek and science, and she joined in endless discussions about literature, Darwin's theories, and the role of women. She helped found a scientific society, and she was president of the literary society. Her Rockford experience spurred self-confidence and encouraged her to excel and to do something significant. She left Rockford and returned to Cedarville in June 1881, having completed the requirements for a B.A., but determined to spend a further year of study at Smith College.

Shortly after returning home Jane became ill and was forced to cancel her plans. Then in August tragedy hit the Addams's family. John Addams died of a ruptured appendix while the family was on a trip in northern Wisconsin.

The death of Jane's father came at a time when she needed his help and guidance most as she searched for direction and purpose after college. The loss of her father increased her confusion about her role as an educated woman. She alone now had to work out the conflicting positions of her "junior exhibition" speech. The impact of her father's death is apparent in a letter she wrote to Ellen:

> I will not write of myself or how purposeless and without ambition I am. Only prepare yourself so you won't be too disappointed in me when you come. The greatest sorrow that can ever come to me has past [sic] and I hope it's only a question of time until I get my moral purpose straightened.

Ellen answered shrewdly: "You are too much like your father, I think, for your moral purpose to be permanently shaken by anything, even the greatest sorrow."

Although Ellen was ultimately right, the years between 1881 and 1889 were a period of unhappiness, illness, mental depression, and aimless travel. In her autobiography Jane wrote, "During most of that time I was absolutely at sea so far as any moral purpose was concerned, clinging only to the desire to live in a really living world and refusing to be content with a shadowy intellectual reflection of it."

Within a few weeks after her father's death, Jane Addams was on her way to Philadelphia, where she enrolled as a student at the Women's Medical College of Pennsylvania. One can only guess why she chose to start medical school at this time. Her stepmother, Anna, did not wish to remain in Cedarville and decided to join her older son and Jane's sister, Alice, who were in Philadelphia for a while. Jane had considered the possibility of medical school while she was at Rockford. It seemed a logical choice for a useful career, and the Women's Medical College of Pennsylvania was one of the earliest of the many women's medical schools that opened in the second half of the nineteenth century.

. Although her father's death had left her well-off and financially independent, Jane left Rockford determined to make herself and her education useful. The difficulty for young women of that period was how to do so. Society had few useful occupations for college-trained women. Only three professions were open to them: teaching, medicine, and nursing. Marriage, the traditional role for women, did not interest Jane. George proposed marriage, and Anna favored it, but for Jane this was out of the question, since she regarded him as a brother. In any case, marriage was an option she seems to have rejected early on.

At that time women believed that it was impossible to combine marriage with a professional career. In later life Jane Addams wrote that "men did not want at first to marry women of the new type, and women could not fulfill the two functions of profession and home-making until modern inventions had made a new type of housekeeping practicable, and . . . until public opinion tolerated the double role."

Teaching was for Jane a possible but not an attractive option. Some of the first generation of college women became teachers in the new women's colleges. On the other hand, the latter part of the nineteenth century was, in some ways, a golden age for women in medicine. Defying the barriers raised against them, women made a concerted effort to enter the medical profession after the Civil War. At first they were trained at one of the women's medical colleges, whose numbers increased rapidly. But by the 1890's several major medical schools were admitting women, and medical schools became coeducational. This development proved unfortunate for women; the white male medical establishment, fearful of overcrowding in the profession, began to force restrictive admission policies on the medical schools.

Before many months at the Women's Medical College, Jane Addams became ill with severe backaches, exhaustion, and depression; she was forced to give up her studies. A few months of S. Weir Mitchell's famous cure for nervous and "invalid" women—total seclusion, rest, and complete inactivity—did not give Jane much relief, and probably only increased her depression. "I have come to the time when I could not read and then found out how much I had depended on that," she wrote.

After returning to Cedarville, she was persuaded by her family and friends to undergo an operation to correct the curvature of her spine. Her brother-in-law, Harry, who was a skilled surgeon, performed the operation. For many months after this operation Jane was bedridden and almost became convinced she was an invalid. She wrote to Ellen, "I was ashamed to show even to my good friends against what lassitude, melancholy and generally crookedness I was struggling." She never returned to medical school. She was convinced that she was a "failure in every sense."

To her sister Alice she wrote a few years later that the problem she faced in Philadelphia was "trying to fulfill too many objects at once." Jane Addams, like many of the college women of her generation, had difficulty in reconciling her career ambitions with conventional family claims. The traditional role of a daughter at home was that of a helper and companion to one's parents. Mrs. Addams expected her stepdaughter to go with her to concerts and museums and to help entertain friends and relatives. Years later Jane Addams was able to generalize from her own experience the dilemma of a whole generation of college women. "It is always difficult for the family to regard the daughter otherwise than a family possession," she wrote. Unlike the situation of the grown-up son who "has so long been considered a citizen with well defined duties and a need of 'making his way in the world' . . . in the case of the grown-up daughter, who is under no necessity of earning a living . . . the years immediately following her graduation from college are too often filled with a restlessness and unhappiness."

Jane Addams realized that college education had started her down a path from which there was no turning back. "Modern woman," she said, "accepts her family claim with loyalty and affection, but she has entered upon a wider inheritance as well, which . . . we call the social claim." When she returns home after four years of college training, the family reasserts its claim. The young woman responds to the best of her ability; once more she becomes preoccupied with domestic affairs. "But where," Addams asked, "is the larger life of which she has dreamed so long?"

Jane Addams saw the young college graduate's conflict between the "family claim" and the "social claim" as a cause not only of unhappiness but even of illness. "When her health gives way under the strain," she wrote, "as it often does, her physician invariably advises a rest. But to be put to bed and fed on milk is not what she requires." For Addams, what was required for the college-educated woman was "common labor," which was the great source of "moral and physical health," and useful work in the world.

Jane enjoyed a respite from illness and depression in a two-year trip to Europe with her stepmother and friends, from 1883 to 1885. The trip was in keeping with her father's educational plan of a grand tour of Europe as the finishing touch to his daughter's education. In the nineteenth century, wealthy parents often provided such a trip for their children; they saw the countries of Europe as the main source of art and learning and wanted their sons and daughters to travel there before settling down to work and marriage. Jane was a more serious student of Europe than the usual American tourist; she studied art intensely, read history books and literature, practiced speaking German, Italian, and French, and carefully observed the people and the sights. In the journal she kept during her trip, there are only brief references to the poor, but in her autobiography written years later, she suggests that her first exposure to urban poverty made a great impression.

The Addams's group stayed briefly in London during October 1883. Their visit occurred about the time when English clergymen and university men from Oxford were discovering and writing about the abject poverty in the city's sprawling city. The poorest people were crowded miserably in the pest-infested squalor of London's East End. Jane wrote her brother that her visit to London was simply a "superficial survey of misery and wretchedness, but it was enough to make one thoroughly sad and perplexed."

In her autobiography she recalled that one of the most painful experiences was being taken by a city missionary to witness the Saturday night sale of rotting vegetables and fruit. "On Mile End Road," she wrote, "from the top of an omnibus, which paused at the end of a dingy street lighted by only occasional flares of gas, we saw two huge masses of ill-clad people clamoring around two hucksters' carts. . . ." Jane took away with her a lasting impression "not of ragged, tawdry clothes nor of pinched and sallow faces, but of myriads of hands, empty, pathetic, nerveless and workworn, showing white in the uncertain light of the street and clutching forward for food that was already unfit to eat."

Addams gained little satisfaction from this European trip: The glimpse of urban poverty merely enhanced her misery. She wrote that she experienced "a sense of futility, of misdirected energy, the belief that the pursuit of cultivation would not in the end bring either solace or relief." She realized with a sense of desolation that modern women, in achieving education, had lost contact with the human condition.

Following her return home Jane hit the bottom in a mood of black despair. She spent winters at home in Baltimore, where her stepmother had moved to accompany her son George, who was attending Johns Hopkins. Here Jane attended lectures, concerts, and parties and helped her stepmother entertain. She found this life empty and purposeless. "I am filled with shame," she wrote to Ellen, "that with all my apparent leisure I have nothing at all to do." At the same time the family claims kept increasing. She was called upon to deal with every new problem which beset the growing Addams family—her brother's illness, the illnesses of her sister Mary or of one of her nieces and nephews.

During a second trip to Europe with Ellen Starr in 1887-1888, Jane went to a meeting of London "match girls" who were on strike. Barely able to live on their wretched wages, the young girls who labored in the match industry faced the prospect of poisoning from the phosphorus with which they constantly worked. The condition resulting from this poisoning was called "phossy jaw" because it affected the jaw and frequently required removing the jawbone.

Meeting the match girls brought Addams to the threshold of a solution to her own personal problem. "It is hard to tell," she said, "just when the very simple plan which afterward developed into the Settlement began to form itself in my mind." Her plan, in essence, was to bring college-educated women together with poor and needy people living in a city. "I gradually became convinced," she wrote, "that it would be a good thing to rent a house in a part of the city where many primitive and actual needs are found." Here young women, "who had been given over too exclusively to study," might learn about life from these people. As educated women, they would be able to apply practically what they had learned from books, and to test the worth of this knowledge in life itself.

As Jane Addams tells it in her autobiography, the moment of decision came in a reaction to her initial indifference to the cruelty of a bullfight she saw in Madrid. Her fascination with the ritual, color, music, uniforms, and blood gave way to sorrow and guilt. She had become indifferent, she told herself, to cruelty and pain and had let her vague idea of doing something about human suffering take the place of any real action. "I had fallen," she wrote, "into the meanest type of self-deception in making myself believe that all this [study and travel] was in preparation for great things to come."

Jane confided her idea of settlement to Ellen Starr. Ellen responded with enthusiasm and expressed a willingness to take part in the experiment. Her reaction convinced Jane that the idea was worth trying and it became "more convincing and tangible although still most hazy in detail."

In the spring of 1888 Jane returned to London and visited Toynbee Hall where her idea became clearer. Toynbee Hall, located in the poorest working-class area of London's East End, was opened in 1884 by a group of Oxford University men. Inspired by the example of Arnold Toynbee, a young Oxford tutor, and encouraged by Samuel Barnett, a Church of England minister in the East End, the founders of Toynbee Hall established the first university settlement as a memorial to Toynbee. Before his untimely death at age thirty-one, Toynbee had done much to proclaim the needs of the poor and the duty of the educated to lead and teach them. As an undergraduate at Oxford University, Toynbee was interested in social issues, particularly the problem of the division of society into rich and poor. In his desire to understand the poor he spent his vacations in the heart of London's East End. He lived in a common lodging house, joined workingmen's clubs, and studied the local organization of charities.

Toynbee believed that one could achieve knowledge of and sympathy for the poor only by living among them and meeting with them on as nearly an equal level as possible. In Whitechapel he met and worked with Samuel Barnett, vicar of St. Jude's parish, who had turned his vicarage into a center for reading, classes, and concerts for area residents. Toynbee's delicate health never permitted another visit to Whitechapel. However, he returned to Oxford with the conviction that the prosperous must know the poor before trying to assist them, and that there would be no progress if men of culture and public spirit did not lead the way. At Oxford he finished his degree, became a tutor, and influenced a good number of undergraduates with his ideas.

After Toynbee's death, Barnett encouraged the establishment of a university colony in East London "where young men who were touched with sympathy for the lives of poorer fellow citizens might live face to face with actual conditions of crowded city life . . . and . . . enoble the lives and improve the material conditions of the people." When Jane Addams visited Toynbee Hall in 1888, fifteen residents—all male university graduates—actively participated in the community, acting as managers of the schools or guardians of the poor.

Toynbee Hall reflected strongly the personality of Canon Barnett, who was the warden of the settlement. Toynbee Hall was not an Episcopalian mission, but it had a decidedly religious motivation. For Barnett, religion was "the one force which can turn the various and often antagonistic classes into fellow workers, making our great cities good for the habitation of both rich and poor." He wrote that "the problem of society seems to be at root a religious problem."

Through the influence of Barnett there was also an emphasis on culture and art at Toynbee Hall. "The poor need more than food," Barnett wrote, "they need also the knowledge, the character, the happiness which are the gifts of God to this Age." The settlement promoted picture exhibitions, concerts, university extension courses, and special lectures. "Toynbee Hall is essentially a transplant of university life in Whitechapel," an American visitor observed.

Toynbee Hall served as a model for Jane Addams in establishing her settlement in Chicago. In 1892, describing the motives for settlement, Jane Addams talked about a "renaissance going forward in Christianity." She saw religion, however, more as a force inspiring people to serve others than as a dogmatic creed. As important as Toynbee Hall was in prompting Jane Addams's idea of a settlement, her insight into her own problem, and that of other college-educated women, in finding a useful and meaningful life also contributed to her settlement plan. Hull-House provided many talented and educated young women with an opportunity "to apply [their] knowledge and theories to life itself and its complicated situations." This gave the Chicago settlement a very different character from Toynbee Hall. As the settlement grew and developed, religious impulses gave way to a quite different set of ideas—to a uniquely American philosophy of social reform.

Culture and education were emphasized at Hull-House just as they were at Toynbee Hall. But the women at Hull-House became more intimately connected with the everyday life of their working-class neighbors. On a day-to-day basis they tried to help them cope with their lives. As the Hull-House women became aware of the problems of their neighborhood, they attempted to deal with them more systematically. With carefully documented reports on inadequate housing and sanitation, infant mortality, and inhuman labor conditions, particularly for women and children, they aroused the public and promoted corrective action by local, state, and national governments. The Chicago settlement, unlike Toynbee Hall, became an effective instrument for social reform led by educated women.

By the turn of the century the settlement idea seemed timely and appropriate to many Americans. Two other settlements had been started in New York, one by women college graduates just a week before Jane Addams and Ellen Starr had established their settlement in Chicago. By 1911 there were four hundred settlements in American cities, thirty-six of them in Chicago alone. The idea of middle-class young people living in poor urban districts came in large part as a response to the shock of the contrast between wealth and poverty that was becoming so apparent in cities across the nation.

4

HULL-HOUSE: The Meaning of Settlement

When Jane Addams and Ellen Starr arrived in Chicago in 1889 to begin their "scheme" of settlement, the city had reached a peak of development after a period of phenomenal growth. It was then the country's second most important manufacturing center, and its leading railroad center. There were over a million residents; four out of every five were foreign-born or the children of immigrants.

George W. Steevens, an English traveler writing of Chicago in 1896, called it "the queen and guttersnipe of cities," a place abounding in huge contrasts of wealth and poverty, filth and beauty, "girdled with a twofold zone of parks and slums; where the keen air from lake and prairie is ever in the nostrils and the stench of foul smoke is never out of the throat. . . . The most American of cities and yet the most mongrel . . . all of which twenty-five years ago . . . was a heap of smoking ashes."

When Jane Addams was born in 1860, Chicago had a population of scarcely 100,000. But the Civil War brought rapid change to its fortunes. Army contractors discovered that Chicago was an ideal location both for the manufacture and distribution of the foodstuffs and clothing that the Army demanded. The livestock market boomed. Corn-fed hogs rolled into Chicago's slaughter-houses by rail to be killed, packed, and speeded on their way to the Army of the West. Wheat, harvested by Chicago's McCormick reapers, poured in, either to be shipped east or to be milled into flour on the spot. Iron production began on a large scale; in 1865 a Chicago plant turned out the first steel rails ever made in the United States. By 1870 the city's population had risen to 300,000; a fine future as a center of culture and a breeder of wealth lay ahead.

The Great Fire of 1871 broke out when Jane Addams was eleven. The story told was that Mrs. Leary's cow kicked over a lantern and started the blaze in the slums of the city's West Side. The fire, which broke out in October, jumped from one tinder-dry wooden shanty to another. Driven by a high wind from the prairies, the flames leaped over the Chicago River, devoured the downtown district, and spread to the wealthy residential areas of the North Side. Two days later the inferno burned itself out. Several hundred people were dead; 100,000 were homeless; and two-thirds of the city lay in ashes.

The disaster shocked the nation and relief poured in. Many believed that Chicago would never rise again. Undaunted by its staggering losses, the city began to rebuild. Some businesses, like the stockyards and packing plants, and grain elevators had been untouched by the fire. Many concerns had been ruined, others began again.

The Chicago that emerged during the 1870's and 1880's boasted more than two hundred millionaires who had made their fortunes in the booming city. They blazoned their success by wearing fine clothes and living in mansions on the exclusive South Side and later on the North Side's lake-front. In 1885 the Potter Palmers set the pace with their English-style granite castle on the lake. It boasted a French drawing room and Gobelin tapestries, a Spanish music room, and a sunken Turkish pool adjoining Mrs. Palmer's Louis XVI bedroom.

The wage earners were the people who had rebuilt Chicago and accomplished the miracle of its economic recovery. During the 1870's and 1880's thousands of Americans, including some fourteen thousand blacks, were drawn from the countryside by the lure of the city's opportunities. Immigrants, too, poured into town; by 1890 they constituted 40 percent of the population, and their children added another 38 percent. Germans, Irish, and Scandinavians were most numerous. There were also Czechs, Poles, Slovaks, Russian Jews, and Italians in smaller numbers.

Most of these immigrants were packed into Chicago's West Side and lived within the great curve formed by the north and south branches of the Chicago River as it flowed toward Lake Michigan. Many of these people toiled in the stockyards that lay to the south or in the shipbuilding yards to the north. The West Side, too, was the heart of Chicago's garment industry.

Chicago's workers lived under miserable conditions, crowded together in one huge unsanitary slum. The city government was corrupt and inefficient; it did little to im-

The tenements in the Nineteenth Ward of Chicago were, for the most part, wooden shacks built for one family but occupied by several.

prove living conditions. As Jane Addams wrote, "The streets are inexpressibly dirty, the number of schools inadequate, sanitation legislation unenforced, the street lighting bad, the paving miserable and altogether lacking in the alleys and smaller streets."

The unpaved streets were dusty in the summer and became, during the rest of the year, mud bogs into which wagons sank to the hubs, and horses to the knees, while drivers cursed and laid on the whip. As for sewage or garbage disposal, the city fathers did not bother about such things. Refuse was dumped into the Chicago River; the city's sewage emptied into the same waters. The *Daily News* indignantly reported that "sewage and garbage of all kinds, animals more or less decomposed, make it reek. . . . " It was small wonder that the drinking water became polluted, and that the death rate from typhoid fever was twice as high as in New York or Boston.

In September 1889 Jane Addams and Ellen Starr came to Chicago to make their home in the heart of the West Side slum. The two women moved into what they would later call Hull-House, a mansion that Charles Hull, a wealthy developer, had built for himself in 1856. In 1880 Hull abandoned his home when the city began to turn what had been a pleasant suburb into a wilderness of tenements and shacks. The house, when Addams arrived, was a run-down but handsome structure with wide verandas set off by stately wooden Corinthian columns. It stood upon Halsted Street, a main thoroughfare that ran right through the West Side on a north-south axis and was lined with butcher shops, saloons, and stores. Hull-House was located in the middle of Chicago's Nineteenth Ward. To the people of this ward, Jane Addams and her companions now planned to devote their lives.

The Nineteenth Ward was a slice of the city bounded by Polk Street on the north, 12th Street on the south, and State Street on the east (see map). It was a community of immigrants: Italians, Polish and Russian Jews, Irish, and Germans. The area of the Nineteenth Ward was little more than one-third of a square mile; it was also probably the

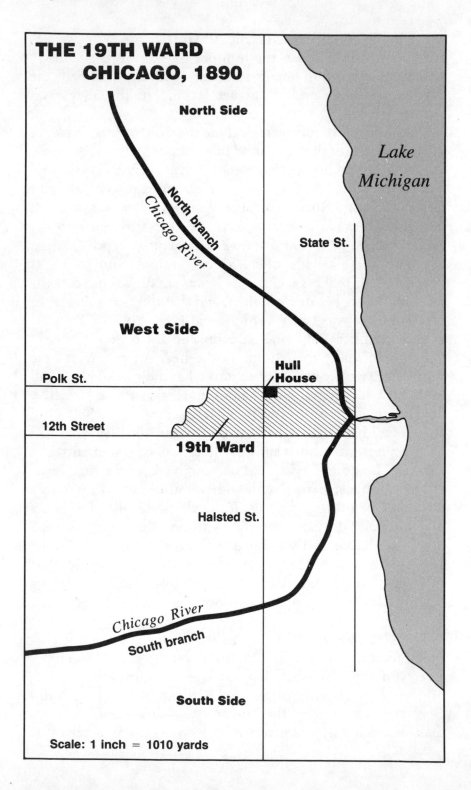

THE 19TH WARD
CHICAGO, 1890

North Side

Lake Michigan

North branch
Chicago River

State St.

West Side

Hull House

Polk St.

12th Street

19th Ward

Halsted St.

Chicago River

South branch

South Side

Scale: 1 inch = 1010 yards

poorest, most crowded section of Chicago. "Little idea can be given," Hull-House staff members reported in 1895, "of the filthy and rotten tenements, the dingy courts and tumble-down sheds, the foul stables and dilapidated outhouses, the broken sewer pipes, the piles of garbage. . . ."

The Nineteenth Ward was alive with children, "filling every nook," as Hull-House observers wrote, "working and playing in every room, eating and sleeping in every window sill, pouring in and out of every door, and seeming literally to pave every scrap of yard. . . ." The mortality of these children was high; the babies appeared starved and pale.

When Jane Addams and Ellen Starr returned from Europe to begin their work among Chicago's immigrants, they had little idea of the reality that would confront them in the Nineteenth Ward. Addams's travels had made her generally aware that there was great poverty in modern cities and a gulf between rich and poor generating bitter conflict. Hull-House was what Addams termed a "settlement," a response to a cry for help, a means of fostering social intercourse between college-trained young women and the very poor, to the advantages of both. "Jane's idea," as Ellen wrote to her sister a few months before she actually moved to Hull-House, "is that settlement is more for the benefit of the people who do it than for the other class." The experience of settlement would soon show them not only how much they would gain but also how much they could contribute.

When Addams and Starr first moved into the Nineteenth Ward, they had no precise idea of exactly what they would be doing. The first task was to get to know their neighbors. The people, understandably, were suspicious and also curious. Why, they asked themselves, would these two rich, well-educated young women want to live among them?

Jane Addams and Ellen Starr at once became involved in the everyday life and problems of the neighborhood. Their actions soon quieted their neighbors' doubts and answered their questions. The people began to think of Hull-House as a haven, a place where they might come for help. "From the first it seemed understood," Addams wrote, "that we were ready to perform the humblest neighborhood services. We were asked to wash the newborn babies and to prepare the dead for burial, to nurse the sick and to mind the children."

Hull-House women did those things, and many more. The settlement, as Addams explained, "resembles a big brother whose mere presence on the playground protects the little ones from bullies." This was especially necessary in the case of abandoned and aged people faced with the ultimate loneliness of the poorhouse.

Addams told of one old woman whom county officers were attempting to drag from her home and take to the infirmary. The poor thing had thrown herself upon a small wooden chest, and was clinging to it like a limpet. "Between her broken gasps for breath," wrote Addams, "she squealed shrilly like a frightened animal caught in a trap. . . . To give an old woman only a chair and a bed, to leave her no cupboard in which her treasures may be stowed, that her mind may dwell upon them in moments of revery, is to reduce living almost beyond the limit of human endurance."

The Nineteenth Ward was the heart of Chicago's garment industry; it was not only a slum but also a den in which both the sweating system and the exploitation of child labor flourished. This reality had much to do with shaping the services that Addams's settlement was called upon to offer.

Garments for the entire clothing trade were cut in large factories in the First Ward, which lay to the east of the Nineteenth Ward, across the river. The cloth, after being cut, was given to "sweaters" to stitch together, then to buttonhole and to hand-finish.

The sweater of the Nineteenth Ward was a middleman; he contracted to deliver finished garments to the factory and hired workers to do the job. The sweater took care to quote a price for the finished work so low that he would likely get the order. He made his profit by driving down the piece rate for those he paid to do the work. He also saved on rent by packing these workers into one filthy room in a tenement, or by letting them take the garments back to their own poorly lit and airless homes.

Sweaters were immigrants who did not shrink from harshly exploiting their neighbors and fellow country people. "An unscrupulous contractor," as Addams wrote, "regards no basement too dark, no stable loft too foul . . . no tenement room too small for his workroom. Hence these shops abound in the worst of the foreign districts where the sweater easily finds his cheap basement and his home finishers."

Wages were so low that parents depended upon their children's pitiful earnings to augment the family income. In many cases, too, fathers became disabled while their children were still small. Employers could drive workers to exhaustion, but they assumed no responsibility if their employees were killed or injured on the job. If the breadwinner lost a limb, or his sight, or his life, the family depended on the mother and children for survival.

Children's work was often dangerous as well as underpaid. Florence Kelley, a Hull-House resident and chief factory inspector for the state of Illinois in 1894, described the conditions of children in the sweatshops. "Many of the boys in these shops," she wrote, "are buttonholers, and every little buttonholer is destined, sooner or later, to develop a curvature of the spine. Other boys run foot-power machines and the doom that awaits them is consumption of the lung or intestine."

Girls as well as boys were employed in these sweatshops. Their backs grew crooked as they sat long hours bent over hemming or sewing on buttons—for a total wage of fifty to eighty cents a week. Like the boys, they operated foot-power machines. But in addition to the diseases suffered by the boys, they also developed pelvic disorders "ruinous," as Kelley said, "to themselves at present and to their children in the future."

These were the people—men, women, and children who worked in the sweatshops and the factories of the Nineteenth Ward—whom Jane Addams and Ellen Starr began to invite to Hull-House as friends and guests. Hull-House quickly became known for its hospitality. Soon there were as many as two thousand visitors a week, many of them women with children.

Before the end of the first month it became clear that there was need for a child-care center. In October a kindergarten with twenty-four children opened in the drawing room downstairs. Jenny Dow, twenty-two-year-old daughter of a leader of the Chicago Woman's Club, volunteered to run it.

Much more was needed, as it turned out, than a kindergarten, which was open only a few hours in the morning. When hard-driven mothers went out to work all day, they often left their tiny children without any care, locked up in a tenement room. The first three crippled children whom Addams encountered in the Nineteenth Ward had all been injured when their mothers were at work: "One had fallen out of a third-story window," she said, "another had been burned, and the third had a curved spine due to the fact that for three years he had been tied all day long to the leg of the kitchen table, ..."

The Hull-House day nursery for children of working mothers developed naturally in response to this situation. "During our first summer," Addams wrote, "these poor little mites would wander into the cool hallway of Hull-House. We kept them there and fed them at noon, in return for which we were sometimes offered a hot penny which had been held in a tight little fist ever since mother left this morning, 'to buy something to eat with.'"

Soon the kindergarten blossomed into a day nursery, with large numbers of children under more systematic supervision. It was located first in a cottage on a side street, then in a building designed for the purpose called the Children's House.

One year after they had launched the settlement, Jane Addams and Ellen Starr had a full program of activities. In the mornings from 9 to 12 the kindergarten met in the long drawing room. In the afternoon they removed the kindergarten furniture, and various clubs and classes used the hall for the rest of the day and evening. Monday afternoons the Italian girls came to sew, play games, and dance. The schoolboy's club met on Tuesday afternoon and the working boy's class met that evening. Some of the boys from the evening class started a Shakespeare class, which grew into a club that met at the settlement for more than twenty years. On Wednesday evenings, the Working People's Social Science Discussion Club had the floor. All working people were invited to hear

Kindergarten children in the settlement front yard.

speakers present their views and then lead discussions on such topics as the eight-hour movement, child labor, and the pros and cons of socialism. Thursday afternoons, a woman doctor talked to neighborhood women on physiology and hygiene and "how to raise healthy children, even near the Chicago River." In addition to these activities, cooking classes were held three times a week in the kitchen. One of the most popular of the Hull-House activities was the social reception held one night each for the French, Germans, and Italians. At these receptions, the language of each group was spoken and entertainment provided. Hull-House had also started college extension courses modeled after those held at Toynbee Hall. These courses consisted of ten weeks of classes taught by college graduates in such subjects as history, languages, political economy, mathematics, and physics.

By the end of 1890 Hull-House had become more than an experiment. The settlement was well on its way to becoming

Hull-House, c. 1892, much the way Jane Addams and Ellen Starr found it in 1889.

a genuine neighborhood center. More than fifty thousand people came through its doors the first year. At the same time, the women who ran Hull-House were becoming experts in the problems of their neighborhood and of the city.

5

HULL-HOUSE: Youth and the Culture of the City

Hull-House grew rapidly. Within a few years there were fifteen young women residing there, and ninety nonresident volunteers. By 1895 the settlement housed twenty residents, both men and women. The residents gave their free time to Hull-House activities and paid their own expenses as well.

From the start Hull-House was experimental. The settlement provided public baths for the neighborhood, and, for a short time, it ran a cooperative coal association. Another experiment was a public kitchen that provided cheap but wholesome food for neighborhood residents. The Butler Art Gallery, built in 1891 as an addition to Hull-House, exhibited masterpieces of Western art. A coffeehouse added in 1893 could not compete with the saloons, but it provided a place for social gatherings. A playground was set up in 1892 and a gymnasium was built in 1893.

Chicago, in twenty years, had risen from the ashes of the Great Fire to become a wealthy city, profiting from the labor of tens of thousands of workers, but feeling no obligation to provide for their safety, happiness, or health.

Jane Addams's vision of a truly humane urban culture was linked with her sensitivity to young people and her sympathy for them. "Industrialism," she said, "has gathered together multitudes of eager young creatures from all quarters of the earth as a labor supply for the countless factories and workshops, upon which the present industrial city is based." The impact of urbanism upon the youth was for her a first concern. This, Addams felt, was the central contradiction of the modern urban experience. "Only in the modern city," she said, "have men concluded that it is no longer necessary for the municipality to provide for the insatiable desire for play."

One set of men, she believed, had organized young people in order to profit from their toil. Another set of men and women, whom she termed "the most evil-minded and unscrupulous members of the community," had established the gin palaces, the saloons, and the dance halls to make money out of youth's unquenchable desire for recreation and for joy.

To treat youth in this way, she believed, is to ignore and to suppress society's most vital and creative force—the rising generation. Youth has a power which will find its outlet. We ignore this fact at our peril. The vast majority of the soldiers who fought in the Civil War, she pointed out, were under twenty-one. Millions of youth in the peacetime world have the same yearning for meaningful action and adventure.

"The most precious moment," she said, "in human development is the young creature's assertion that he is unlike any other human being, and has an individual contribution to make to the world. . . ." What might we do with youth's ideals and its energies if we could harness those millions of individual contributions to help transform the modern city, to make it, as she put it, "a more beautiful, more companionable place in which to live?"

The spirit of youth with its joy and creativity was alive in the city streets. However, that spirit found expression in distorted forms, such as building fires along the railroad tracks or stealing apples from a freight car. "The stupid experiment," wrote Addams, "of organizing work but failing to organize play, has brought about its own revenge. . . . The love of pleasure will not be denied, and when it has turned into all sorts of malignant and vicious appetites, then we, the middle-aged, . . . resort to all sorts of restrictive measures."

Years of experience at Hull-House gave Addams an intimate knowledge of the dangers that beset Chicago youth and made her familiar with the tragedies of many young people. She gave some account of these case histories in her book, *The Spirit of Youth and the City Streets*, published in 1909.

A few children were what Addams called "tramp boys," rebellious souls, for whom the search for excitement took a simple form; they fled the city and became vagrants or nomads, roaming the countryside and the wide world.

She cited the case of one such boy, a true adventurer. Between the ages of eleven and fifteen he "travelled almost around the world." No monotonous factory work for him! How the child lived was a mystery; Addams appreciated his courage and self-reliance. The young man eventually wound up in Chicago again where, she tells us, "skillful efforts [were] made to detain him." These were in vain. He once more started on his travels, "throwing out such hints as that of 'a trip into Old Mexico,' or 'following up Roosevelt into Africa.'"

For most Chicago youth the option of such traveling was nonexistent. Most of their deeds of adventure were of a lesser sort: throwing stones at moving trains, switching switches and derailing street cars, setting fires, vandalizing signs and cutting cables, shoplifting, and stealing horses and buggies for joy rides.

These delinquencies brought the young people before the courts. Thousands of them were arrested every year. Here Addams underlined a significant fact. "Practically the whole machinery of the grand jury and the criminal courts," she charged, "is maintained and operated for the benefit of youths between 13 and 25." Many of the offenses for which the young had been charged were crimes of great imagination, carried out with recklessness and bravado. Few adults could have committed them. "Only the [use] of that sudden burst of energy belonging partly to the future could have achieved them," wrote Addams, "only the capture of the imagination and of the deepest emotion of youth could have prevented them."

A chief form of recreation for young people in Chicago in the 1890's was the lurid, five-cent commercial theater. "Going to the Show," wrote Addams, "is [their] only possible road to the realms of mystery and romance." This love of the theater was, in part, a search for distraction and an escape from the grim realities of the working child's daily life. Children would get hold of money for the theater in any way they could. "Out of my twenty years experience at Hull-House," she wrote, "I can recall all sorts of pilferings, petty larcenies and even burglaries, due to the never ceasing effort on the part of boys to procure theater tickets."

The theater attracted young people because it expressed basic feelings of love, jealousy, and revenge, and because it kindled the youthful imagination through its portrayal of daring acts. Night after night these theaters unfolded "the most improbable tales" before their youthful audiences. Hundreds of young people, she wrote, "model their conduct upon the standards set before them on this mimic stage."

The theater at the end of the nineteenth century was becoming the most popular teacher of public morality, as any attendance survey of Chicago's churches and theaters would show. The theater, Addams agreed with an English playwright, "is literally making the minds of our urban population. . . . [It] is not only a place of amusement, it is a place of culture, a place where people learn how to think, act and feel." It was an educational force more powerful than the public schools themselves.

The consequences of these theatrical lessons were soon evident upon Chicago's streets. Addams told of one incident which took place in the Nineteenth Ward. Three boys, aged nine, eleven, and thirteen years, had recently visited the theater and were entertained with a story of frontier life. The play included a stagecoach holdup with the lassoing of the driver.

These children decided to undertake a similar adventure. They saved enough money to buy a revolver and spent weeks planning to lasso, murder, and rob a neighborhood milkman. Their motto was "Dead men tell no tales." One morning "the conspirators, with their faces covered with black cloth, lay in ambush for the milkman. Fortunately for him, as the lariat was thrown the horse shied, and although the shot was fired the milkman's life was saved."

By the 1890's, the West was linked in the youthful mind with the cheap heroics of gunplay. "An entire series of difficulties," Addams said, was "directly traceable to the foolish and adventurous [practice] of carrying loaded firearms." Numbers of young people in Chicago carried guns. Hardly a day passed when the papers did not record shootings. "What might be merely a boyish scrap," she said, "is turned into a tragedy because some boy has a revolver."

In one case, a young man who had been born on a small farm in Ohio was sentenced to death for killing a policeman as the boy was being arrested for a minor offense. "Davie was never a bad boy," said his mother, "until about five years ago when he began to go with this gang who are always looking out for fun."

American immigrants during the late nineteenth century were often targets of hatred and prejudice by people who had immigrated earlier. Many immigrants, too, came from parts of Europe that had been torn for centuries by bitter rivalries—Gentile against Jew, Magyar and German against Slav, Balkan and Armenian peoples against their Turkish oppressors.

Some Chicago children, in their search for a heroic life and a cause, joined in these antagonisms. "I remember a Greek boy of fifteen," wrote Addams, "stirred by some vague notion of carrying on a traditional warfare, and of adding another page to the heroic annals of Greek history." He had been arrested for threatening to hang a young Turkish lad. The court let him go with a caution. The child was "covered with confusion and remorse that he had brought disgrace upon the name of Greece when he had hoped to add to its glory."

For a number of years Hull-House residents battled the traffic in drugs. "The long effort," wrote Addams, "brought us into contact with dozens of boys who had become victims of the cocaine habit." Some of these boys ran in gangs, lived the life of jobless vagrants, and had their clubhouses on abandoned, garbage-strewn lots. One such gang—all clothed in rags—was brought to Hull-House in critical condition. Some of its members were emaciated and all were seriously addicted.

The desire to dream, Addams thought, to see visions, to escape a poverty-stricken existence, played an important part in these young people becoming hooked on cocaine. One gang used a small hut for its retreat. "When they had accumulated enough [dope] for a real debauch they went to this hut and for several days were dead to the outside world." One child told Addams that in his dreams he saw "large rooms paved with gold and silver money, the walls papered with greenbacks, and that he took away in buckets all that he could carry."

Jane Addams not only wrote about the needs of youth; she also attempted to meet those needs at Hull-House. The settlement clubs, social centers for the young, constantly held dances and parties. The Hull-House Players, established in 1901, provided an opportunity for its young members to take part in drama, and offered an alternative theater experience for the young people.

Hull-House also established the first public playground in Chicago in 1892. A sand pile, swings, building blocks, and a slide served the needs of the younger children, while the older boys had an area for playing handball and baseball. A member of the Hull-House community and a city policeman supervised the playground.

These private efforts provided a model for a larger public effort to create recreational facilities in Chicago. In fact, Hull-House and other Chicago settlements provided much of the experience needed for building the city's park system. Edward B. DeGroot, for example, moved from his post as Hull-House playground leader to the Director of Gymnastics and Athletics for the South Park District. Settlement workers also helped to found the Playground Association of America in order to promote their ideas about recreation throughout the country.

Successful experiments like the playground, Addams believed, should become publicly supported. "There are many things," she wrote in 1892, "which the public would never do unless they were first supplied by individual initiative. . . . Each social experiment is thus tested by a few people, and given wide publicity . . . before the public prudently makes up its mind whether or not it is wise to incorporate it into the functions of government."

Jane Addams not only developed models for a humane urban community, but she also saw what was wrong with existing public programs. She had little patience with the public education system as it existed in Chicago during the 1890's. Throughout the country at that time, educational systems

The first public playground in Chicago was started by Hull-House in 1893.

sought to "assimilate" the immigrant youth. They saw their mission to turn immigrant children into good Americans by teaching them to recite the Pledge of Allegiance, to read, write, and speak English, and to take pride in George Washington and the American past.

Public school education of that day was, in fact, arid and inhuman, based upon rote and recitation, and remote from the daily lives of the young and their problems. At school children learned to despise the language of their parents, while they learned little to prepare them for the new industrial world in which they would spend their lives.

Addams came to realize the impact of industrialization upon her neighbors, and to question any cultural or educational program that did not take this into account. She began to understand some of the implications of the settlement's programs through a fruitful relationship with John Dewey, the philosopher and educational reformer. Dewey was a frequent visitor to Hull-House after he arrived at the newly established University of Chicago in 1892.

By the end of the 1830's Addams had come to question the value of the college extension courses that she had introduced so eagerly in the settlement's early days. She found the approach in many ways too academic; the subjects taught were remote from the life and experience of her neighbors. "We fail," she wrote, "to realize that because we are living in an industrial age we must find our culture through that industry, and that to seek culture in some other age than our own is to wear a borrowed, ill-fitting garment."

Addams, therefore, began to experiment with a different approach by establishing the Hull-House Labor Museum.

The idea for this museum arose out of Addams's concern about the relationship between the immigrants and their children. "An overmastering desire to reveal the humbler immigrants parents to their own children," she wrote, "lay at the base of [this]."

The idea came to her while she was watching an old Italian woman spinning with the simple stick spindle—a weighted stick attached to a roving of unspun yarn. Surely, Addams thought, Hull-House ought to be able to set up some kind of demonstration to show the connection between the ancient style of handspinning and the whirring, clacking, spinning machines that immigrant children were operating in Chicago's factories. In this way, it might be possible "to build a bridge between European and American experiences."

The children needed to be taught the intimate connection between the old ways and the new in order to give them the ability, as Addams put it, "to see life as a whole." The lack of this ability, in her view, was "the most fruitful source of misunderstanding between European immigrants and their children, as it is between them and their American neighbors."

Addams set up spinning and weaving exhibits at Hull-House. Syrian, Greek, Italian, Russian, and Irish women showed how handspinning and handweaving had been done in the Old World. The demonstrations were accompanied by lectures on industrial history that explained how the American factory system inherited these old techniques, took them out of the human hand, and attached them to power-driven machines.

Garment workers thronged to these lectures, which were given in the evenings. One worker remarked to Addams that she didn't think of them as lectures. She called them "getting next to the stuff you work with all the time."

Addams understood the importance of teaching young people the nature of the industrial revolution, which, within the span of a single century, had transformed the American world. Here she showed herself to be an educational pioneer far in advance of her time.

Jane Addams had her own vision of what a city and its culture ought to be. Cities are places, she said, quoting the Greek philosopher Aristotle, "where men have a common life for noble ends." But the culture and civilization of the city depends on the community's providing recreation for all of its inhabitants. Play will unite city dwellers, drawing them into companionship, which both reveals and respects human differences. Just like the cities of ancient Greece, she believed, the modern city needs its public games like the modern sport of baseball; which, she happily noted, "the theater even now by no means competes with."

Addams was encouraged as she surveyed in 1909 the changes that had taken place in Chicago since Hull-House had opened. "Boston has its gymnasiums, cricket fields, and golf courses," she wrote, "Chicago has seventeen parks . . . which at present enroll thousands of young people. . . ." But it was not enough. "We are only beginning," she wrote, "to understand what might be done through the festival, the street procession, the band of marching musicians, orchestral music in public squares or parks, with the magic power they all possess to formulate the sense of companionship and solidarity."

6

HULL-HOUSE: Community of Reformers

While Jane Addams was developing her radical critique of the modern commercial city and seeking new methods for the creation of an urban community, the Hull-House settlement was itself becoming an unusual community in the heart of the immigrant working-class district of Chicago. It was a community of diverse nationalities and individuals of every class and generation. Much of the settlement's activities served as bridges between groups isolated by class, generation, and nationality. And it was rapidly becoming a commmunity of reformers, linking prominent and wealthy citizens with the immigrants and working class of Chicago in efforts to achieve social change.

The young women at Hull-House, wanting to open the lines of communication between the classes, joined the struggles of their neighbors in order to make their settlement a real community enterprise. "We quickly discovered," wrote Addams, "that nothing brought us so absolutely into comradeship with our neighbors as mutual and sustained efforts such as the paving of a street, the closing of a gambling house, or the restoration of a veteran policeman." The Hull-House women soon became fighters for labor legislation, union rights, adequate medical care for children, and decent housing.

From their arrival in Chicago, Jane Addams and Ellen Starr had appreciated the importance of obtaining the support of Chicago's social, religious, and civic leaders. They were particularly successful in gaining the help of a number of women who belonged to the Chicago Woman's Club. The club offered the wives of wealthy and prominent Chicago businessmen intellectual stimulation through its lectures, as well as a feeling of usefulness through civic improvement projects. Some of the club leaders were so impressed with Jane Addams when she presented her idea of a settlement, that they immediately invited her to become a member. The Woman's Club lent powerful support to the settlement by declaring it socially acceptable. Soon daughters of Chicago's more prominent citizens were volunteering their services to the settlement. Addams's connection with the Woman's Club gave Hull-House an important political link to powerful members of Chicago society who would be key to the success of its later reform efforts.

Hull-House quickly became, as the journalist Henry Demarest Lloyd called it, "the best club" in Chicago. It attracted a lot of visitors, many of whom became friends and allies for its causes, and some of whom became active members of the Hull-House community. For example, the wealthy and commanding Mrs. Louise DeKoven Bowen was an officer of the Hull-House Woman's Club for seventeen years. This organization, modeled on the more elite Chicago Woman's Club, was formed for immigrant women on Chicago's West Side.

The relationship with various reformers, trade union leaders, and the Chicago Woman's Club was crucial to the success of the Hull-House women in battling for the causes of their community. The most important element in the settlement's success, however, was the remarkable group of young residents attracted to the settlement by the personality of Jane Addams. She had a unique ability to create a sense of unity and commitment among talented and strikingly individual personalities. Although there were impressive male residents, it was the extraordinary group of women at Hull-House that made it famous and influential.

In the beginning the Hull-House community consisted only of Jane Addams and Ellen Starr who, over the years, had developed a relationship of love and mutual dependency. After the establishment of Hull-House, Ellen Starr gradually moved into the background of Jane's life. However, she always made Hull-House her home and played an important role in its activities and administration.

Soon after its establishment, the settlement expanded rapidly as new residents arrived. One of the earliest was Julia Lathrop, whose background was similar to Jane Addams's. She was the daughter of a prominent lawyer from Rockford, Illinois, who, as an ardent antislavery advocate, had helped to organize the Republican Party in Illinois and served both in the state legislature and in Congress. He believed in equal rights for women and encouraged his daughter in her interest in public affairs. Julia's mother, an advocate of woman suffrage, was a member of the first graduating class at Rockford Female Seminary. Julia had attended the seminary for one year before going off to Vassar to finish her college education. Returning to Rockford in 1880, Julia did not know quite what to do with her education. For ten years she lived at home and read law in her father's law office while serving as his secretary. In 1889 she heard Jane Addams speak about Hull-House at Rockford College and she decided to join the settlement.

In appearance, Julia was small and quite plain with prominent features and a somewhat mournful expression. However, she had great vitality and warmth, a dry wit, and she appreciated the comic side of life. Francis Hackett, a young resident who lived several years at Hull-House, gave the following description of her:

> In the third month of my residence, I was told 'Miss Lathrop is coming! Miss Lathrop is coming!' as if it were an occasion for

public rejoicing. . . . I did not know Miss Julia Lathrop of Rockford, Illinois, who brought with her such force, such warmth, such an almost roguish sense of the tragi-comedy of American politics. You felt she enjoyed the game without losing sight for one moment of the big end she had in view. Her brown eyes, so sincere but with a sparkle lurking in them, her slow redolent voice, her flavor of Illinois, gave her a richness which was valued by colleagues who had less vitality.

In the early days of the settlement, Julia Lathrop and Jane Addams had a number of adventures as they tried to meet the crises of the neighborhood. At one point they found themselves midwives at the birth of an illegitimate child. After the baby was born, Jane Addams remarked, "This doing things that we don't know how to do is going too far. Why did we let ourselves be rushed into midwifery?" To which Julia Lathrop replied, "If we have to begin to hew down to the line of our ignorance, for goodness' sake don't let us begin at the humanitarian end." The two young women were called upon to handle many crises in their neighborhood despite their inexperience. Once they rescued horses from a stable that had caught fire. For Julia Lathrop it was impossible to plead ignorance and inexperience if a neighborhood crisis involved a human being.

In later years both Jane Addams and Julia Lathrop would be too busy for this kind of adventure. In 1893 Governor John Peter Altgeld appointed Julia to the Illinois Board of Charities. Visiting the county farms and poorhouses of the state, she became an expert on public welfare. She objected to the indiscriminate grouping of the young, the old, the sick, and insane in the same institutions and the staffing of the institutions with unqualified political appointees. She fought for the nonpolitical appointment of qualified experts to staff the state institutions, specifically trained social workers. Two younger residents of Hull-House, Sophonisba Breckinridge and Edith Abbot, helped realize Lathrop's goal by training a whole generation of social workers at the country's first professional school of social work, the Chicago School of Civics and Philanthropy that Lathrop had helped to found.

Two groups of inmates in state institutions became Lathrop's special concern, the mentally ill and juvenile delinquents. She tried to create public awareness about the nature and treatment of mental illness. She also led efforts to enact a law setting up in 1899 the first juvenile court in the country, enlisting the help of the Chicago Woman's Club and the Chicago Bar Association. The law provided for the appointment of probation officers, but the legislature provided no money. So Julia organized the Juvenile Court Committee to appoint and raise the salaries for probation officers and to provide a detention home and psychopathic clinic at the juvenile court.

In 1912 Julia was appointed head of the new U.S. Children's Bureau, the establishment of which owed a great deal to the efforts of another Hull-House resident, Florence Kelley. During her tenure at the Children's Bureau, Julia Lathrop supervised investigations into infant and maternal mortality, nutrition, juvenile delinquency, and child labor. In 1916, after the first child labor law was passed by Congress, she brought another young Hull-House resident, Grace Abbott, to the bureau to take charge of law enforcement. At the end of Lathrop's career at the bureau, one of her long-standing goals was finally achieved. In 1921 Congress passed the Sheppard-Towner Act, which provided federal aid to states that would set up prenatal and child-health centers in order to reduce the high rate of infant and maternal mortality.

More than any other person at Hull-House, Florence Kelley galvanized Hull-House residents into political action for social reform. Florence Kelley arrived at Hull-House in late 1891 in need of a home and a way to support herself and her three children. Jane Addams gave her room and board and a job at Hull-House running an experimental employment office for working girls.

Although Florence Kelley's background was similar to that of Jane Addams, her personality and the life she had led after college were different. Like Jane Addams and Julia Lathrop, Florence Kelley had a close relationship with a politically active father who encouraged his daughter in her education and in her interest in public affairs. William Kelley, a self-educated man, achieved prosperity and prominence as a lawyer and then as a judge in Philadelphia. In the 1850's he became active politically in opposing the extension of slavery, and he became early involved in the Republican Party, supporting Lincoln's candidacy for president. Elected to Congress as a Republican, Kelley was a close friend of Lincoln during his presidency.

Florence was frequently ill as a child, but with her father's encouragement and the use of his library, she made up for the interruptions in her formal schooling and prepared herself to enter Cornell University, which had become coeducational in 1874. Florence was one of the pioneer women at Cornell, where she began her study of law, economics, and history. After graduation she applied to the University of Pennsylvania graduate school. She was refused admission on the ground that she was a woman. While in Europe caring for her brother, who was recovering from an illness, she learned that the University of Zurich admitted women for higher degrees. She enrolled to study economics and law.

In the early 1880's Zurich was a haven for European socialists. Florence converted to socialism and read extensively the works of the socialist Karl Marx and his collaborator Frederick Engels. Concerned that Americans knew little about scientific socialism because so few of the works of Marx and Engels had been published in the United States, she wrote to Engels. She proposed to translate into English his classic study of the horrors of early industrialism, *The Condition of the Working Class in England in 1844*, for publication in the United States. He agreed to her proposal, and her translation marked the beginning of a continuing friendship with Engels, kept up largely through correspondence.

During her two years at Zurich, Florence married a fellow socialist, a Polish-Russian medical student. In 1886 Kelley and her husband returned to New York with their first child. Two other children were born during their years in New York while her husband attempted unsuccessfully to establish a medical practice. Kelley and her husband joined the Socialist Labor Party in New York City, but were expelled as a result of inner party squabbles.

In New York Florence continued her translation of socialist works with a pamphlet by Marx on free trade. She began writing about child labor—a subject to which she would dedicate her energies for the rest of her life. She also helped to organize working women and to improve the conditions of women's work through legislation.

Thus, the pattern of Kelley's lifetime work was already clear by the time that she separated from her husband and came to Chicago with her three children. "We have a colony," she wrote to Engels a few months after her arrival, "of efficient and intelligent women living in a workingmen's quarter, with the house used for all sorts of purposes by about a thousand persons a week. . . . Next week we are to take the initiative in a systematic endeavor to clear out the sweating dens." Kelley informed Engels that she was conducting a women's labor bureau, and that she was "learning more in a week of the actual conditions of proletarian life in America than in any previous year."

Throwing herself into the Chicago campaign for factory legislation, Kelley challenged Addams and the other Hull-House residents to take "a more intelligent interest in the industrial conditions around them." Kelley, indeed, was one of the more radical of the independent women of the late nineteenth century. Edith Abbott, another Hull-House resident, wrote of Kelley that "she brought magnificent weapons to bear on the enemy. Sleepless, tireless, indefatigable, she was always on the alert. Life was never dull and the world was never indifferent where she lived and moved."

Alice Hamilton was one of the young residents of Hull-House who, during the 1890's, became part of Jane Addams's inner circle. The Hamiltons were an established, privileged, and cultured family in the small town of Ft. Wayne, Indiana. Alice's grandfather was a successful entrepreneur and builder of the Hamilton fortune. Alice's father, unsuccessful in business, eventually retreated to his library. He took a deep interest in his daughters' education and, in their early years, was their principal educator. Alice's mother was warm and sympathetic, yet she did not dominate her children. She encouraged them to pursue their own goals and talents. From her mother, Alice later wrote, she came to understand that "personal liberty [is] the most precious thing in life."

In 1892 Alice left her home to attend medical school at the University of Michigan. After working at two women's hospitals, she decided not to become a doctor, but to pursue a scientific career. She went abroad to continue her studies of bacteriology and pathology at Leipzig, Germany, although she could not get an advanced degree because she was a woman. She arrived at Hull-House in 1897, having been offered a position teaching pathology at the Woman's Medical School at Northwestern University. In her spare time she ran a well-baby clinic at the settlement.

When the Woman's Medical School closed, Alice began to devote her energies to the study of industrial diseases, such as "phossy jaw" which Jane Addams had first learned about at a meeting of London match girls in 1887. In 1909 Alice Hamilton was appointed by the governor of Illinois to the Illinois Commission on Occupational Diseases. She became the medical investigator for a survey on lead poisoning, which the commission recommended. Lead was widely used in industry, causing a high toll in illness and death. In severe cases victims suffered from convulsions and temporary blindness. The poison also injured the nervous system, causing paralysis and premature senility.

Alice Hamilton soon became the first and foremost expert in industrial medicine, a fact Harvard Medical School later recognized by making her its first woman faculty member. Continuing her investigations, she was responsible for the improvement of safety requirements in a number of industries. As her biographer, Barbara Sicherman, wrote, "At a time when the federal government lacked enforcement power, she assumed personal responsibility for persuading owners to reform the conditions she brought to light."

Mary Roset Smith was one of several upper-class young ladies in Chicago who was attracted to Hull-House in its first years. She was a friend of Jenny Dow and for a time helped out in the kindergarten. Although she never became a resident or an associate in Hull-House reform, she supported the Hull-House community, and her friendship was very special to Jane Addams. Sensitive, considerate, and generous, Mary could always be depended on whenever material needs arose, whether it was providing gifts for the neighborhood children at Christmas, money for tuition for the children of Florence Kelley, or a check to tide the settlement through a financial crisis.

During the 1890's, the friendship between Jane Addams and this tall, slender, and beautiful young woman grew closer. Jane Addams came to depend on Mary's affection and companionship. Mary was the one friend with whom she could discuss her problems at Hull-House. It was to Mary that she wrote about her financial difficulties, the strain of which plagued her in the early years of Hull-House. For in spite of all Addams's other activities, she alone shouldered the responsibility to keep Hull-House a going concern. She paid the expenses of Hull-House from her own pocket, but its rapid growth strained her comparatively modest income. She had to turn to other sources of support, which, in time, she became skillful in attracting. Jane did not always save Mary's letters in reply to her complaints about lack of money for needed programs. However, it is clear that Mary responded generously. "The check came this afternoon," Jane Addams wrote in 1894. "It gives me a lump in the throat to think of the round thousand dollars you have put into the prosaic bakery and the more prosaic debt when there are so many more things you might have done and wanted to do. It grieves me a little lest our friendship (which is really a very dear thing to me) would be buried by all those money transactions."

Mary's home in Chicago became a second home for Jane when she needed a refuge from Hull-House. In 1895 she spent many weeks there cared for by Mary and her family after an illness of typhoid fever. Mary's affection and attention became more important to Jane as she became a public figure. When Jane went on speaking tours around the country, Mary frequently accompanied her. They spent time together every summer in Maine, where they had bought a cottage. In Maine Jane found time to write, as well as to rest. These weeks refreshed her and enabled Jane to devote her full energies to the work in Chicago for the rest of the year.

Other women of different backgrounds joined the Hull-House community in those early years. Alzina Parsons Stevens and Mary Kenny became residents in the early 1890's and brought to the group their experience in the woman's labor movement in Chicago.

Alzina was born in Parsonsfield, Maine, which had been founded by her grandfather on land received for his service as commander of the Massachusetts regiment in the Revolutionary War. After the death of her father, a relatively prosperous farmer, Alzina's family lost everything and she was forced to work in a New England textile mill at the age of thirteen. At work she lost her right index finger when she tried to clean the space behind her loom while the machine was running "because the looms were running ten hours a day and to clean when the looms stopped meant going to the mills before 6:30 in the morning."

In 1866 Alzina left the textile mill. The wage reductions, she wrote, were "so frequent and excessive that self-respecting American girls, who wished to live the rational life of human beings, were finally forced out of the mills entirely and compelled to seek new fields of industry." This was a different world from the early days of the New England textile industry in the 1830's. At that time Lowell, Massachusetts, was known as a model factory town. Young country women, who worked in the mills for a few years before marrying, went to lectures in the evenings and put out their own literary magazine.

In 1872 Alzina appeared in Chicago where she learned the printing trade and became the first woman admitted to a union covering her craft. In 1877 she founded the Working Woman's Union, which became a female local of the new national labor organization, the Knights of Labor. Working with other women labor activists, like Elizabeth Morgan and Lucy Parsons, Alzina organized working women and played an active role in the labor struggles of the 1880's. She was particularly active in the long and militant campaign for the eight-hour day, which culminated in the Haymarket Massacre. This event followed the attempt by police to break up a labor meeting in Haymarket Square in 1886. A bomb, thrown from the crowd, exploded among the front line of police, who then opened fire. Several police officers were killed and both police and bystanders were wounded.

Mary Kenny reluctantly came to Hull-House in response to an invitation to dinner from Jane Addams. A tall, red-haired Irish girl from a working-class background, she at first regarded the residents of the settlement as "rich and not friends of the worker." She was soon persuaded otherwise by Jane Addams's concrete offers of help; Hull-House became a meeting place for the bookbinder's union which Kenny had organized. Mary Kenny came to live at the settlement. In 1891 with Jane Addams's help, she established the Jane Club, a cooperative women's residence where working girls could live comfortably and cheaply without fear of eviction when engaged in a strike.

Mary Kenny had arrived in Chicago some years earlier with her invalid mother, whom she had helped to support since the age of fourteen. She progressed through the ranks of the printing trade before she began to organize workers in the printing industry. Her method was to move from shop to shop in order to unionize them. She joined the Ladies Federal Labor Union (LFLU), which had been chartered in 1888 by the American Federation of Labor (AFL) as an occupationally mixed women's union.

In 1893 the Hull-House women embarked on their first successful campaign to right social ills, to expose the evils of Chicago's "sweating dens," as Florence Kelley called them, and to limit by law the working hours of women and children.

Early in 1892, just after Florence Kelley arrived in Chicago, a pamphlet by labor activist Elizabeth Morgan caused a sensation by exposing the sweatshop conditions in the garment industry. Kelley soon investigated the sweatshops herself.

Proposing that the state of Illinois make a formal investigation of the sweating system, she was appointed in May to do the study.

Conditions in Chicago, as well as those in other poor districts of large American cities, had by this time attracted the attention of the federal government. That same spring of 1892, Representative Sherman Hoar came to Chicago from Washington, D.C., to investigate labor conditions. Florence Kelley and Elizabeth Morgan conducted his sweatshop tour and also testified before his investigating committee. This caused a furor in the press and also gave national publicity to sweatshop conditions in Chicago.

Prodded into action, the Illinois legislature appointed in January 1893 its own commission to inquire into the employment of women and children in industry. When the commission members arrived at Chicago in February 1893, Florence Kelley was their guide. The commission, she wrote, was intended "as a sop to labor . . . a protracted junket to Chicago for a number of rural legislators." The visitors were overwhelmed by the hospitality of the Hull-House women, who made sure that the legislators saw everything and that their investigation was both thorough and successful. Kelley said that this attention "though irksome in the extreme to the lawmakers, ended in a report so compendious, so readable, so surprising, that they presented it with pride to the legislature."

Kelley did much more than show the legislators around. With the help of Abraham Bisno, a veteran organizer in the garment district, Henry Demarest Lloyd, and a number of prominent lawyers, she drafted an effective antisweatshop bill for the commission to take back to the state capitol.

In June 1893 the Illinois legislature passed Kelley's bill almost without opposition. Its success was due to the community campaigns organized by Hull-House, to the trade unions, and to reformers like Henry Demarest Lloyd. An appeal was made, as Jane Addams explained, "to all elements of the community, and a little group of us addressed the open meetings of trade-unions and benefit societies, church organizations and social clubs literally every evening for three months." Addams insisted, too, that well-known Chicago women should accompany the settlement people and the trade unionists who lobbied for the passage of the bill in Springfield.

The law was a pioneering effort. It regulated sanitary conditions in the sweatshops, fixed fourteen as the minimum age for child employment in manufacture, and prescribed eight hours as the maximum for women and children to work. The law also called for the appointment of twelve inspectors to enforce its provisions.

Governor Altgeld appointed Florence Kelley as chief factory inspector. With Alzina Stevens as her assistant and Mary Kenny as a deputy, Kelly set an example of rigid enforcement of labor laws that was unheard of at the time. Hull-House supported this effort. Although organized labor had supported the factory legislation, opposition had come from parents who feared that the loss of their children's wages would mean starvation for the family. Some parents did not realize that child labor depressed adult wages and that, in the long run, the standard of living of families with working children would be improved if the children stopped working. Jane Addams tried to help those families who were deprived of wages because of the new law. "The sense that the passage of the child labor law," she wrote:

> would in many cases work hardship, was never absent from my mind during the earliest years of its operation. I addressed as many mother's meetings and clubs among working women as I could in order to make clear the objective of the law and the ultimate benefit to themselves as well as to their children.

The Hull-House women's success was short-lived. In 1895 the Illinois Manufacturing Association, formed expressly to fight the eight-hour law, won a victory when the Illinois courts declared it to be unconstitutional. Political appointees replaced Florence Kelley and her associates as factory inspectors. Nonetheless, in a short time, Kelley and her inspectors had shown what could be done by the vigorous enforcement of reform laws. They proved that women could use the power of the state to carry out change.

The campaign for factory legislation in 1893 moved Jane Addams into the political arena with a deepened commitment to reform.

7

CHICAGO: The White City, the Black City

1893 was a year of sharp contrast in Chicago. While the women at Hull-House embarked on their campaign for factory legislation to improve labor conditions, Chicago prepared to host the World's Columbian Exposition, marking the four hundredth anniversary of Columbus's voyage to the New World. All winter work went forward to create a magnificent "White City" on the shores of Lake Michigan, five miles south of the business district. As the steel frames for the great buildings were erected they were covered by elaborate ornamental walls. The walls were then coated with stucco, which was painted white with gold trim.

The fair made an enormous impression on the more than twenty million people who saw it. Hamlin Garlin, a young writer soon to be famous, wrote his aging parents at their Dakota farm: "Sell the cook stove if necessary and come. You *must* see this fair."

The exposition opened on May 1, 1893. An enthusiastic and unruly crowd, estimated at nearly half-a-million people, thronged into the Court of Honor and gazed admiringly at the dome of the Administration Building, which was higher than the dome of the nation's Capitol. President Grover Cleveland, cabinet members, royalty from Spain, and Illinois' new governor, John Peter Altgeld, arrived in their carriages. The president praised the exposition as the "stupendous result of American enterprise." He pushed a button and thousands of flags unfurled. Guns boomed from the warships on Lake Michigan.

All during the summer scholarly meetings on juvenile delinquency, crime prevention, and suffrage reform were held at the new Art Institute. A small group gathered for a conference of settlement workers who came from cities like Boston and New York to meet with their Chicago colleagues. Addams, who did much to bring about this meeting, found herself a leader of a national settlement movement.

The immediate triumph of the exposition was short-lived. A financial panic had struck the American business world in the early spring, marking the beginning of a four-year depression. In Chicago, the depression was staved off for a time as the exposition drew a stream of visitors to spend their money. But even during the summer there was already an unusually high number of unemployed, many of them former construction workers at the fairgrounds.

"The White City . . . constructed only for a season and finished to the minutest detail, must disappear forever, while the black city, which will endure forever, is only at its commencement," wrote a departing journalist in December 1893. Already visitors to the fair had become acquainted with part of the "Black City." Chicago with its saloons, gambling houses, and brothels did a particularly good business in the summer of 1893. By the end of the fair, Chicago was truly a black city as she experienced the depression of "that terrible winter after the World's Fair." Desperate men and women—jobless, homeless, hungry, and cold from the bitter winds off Lake Michigan—held huge demonstrations, reminding Jane Addams of "the London gatherings in Trafalgar Square." The unemployed and homeless poured into the county poorhouse. They fought for space on the floors of police stations and the city hall where they made "a pavement of human bodies . . . pigged together literally like herrings in a barrel," according to William T. Stead, a British journalist.

Stead had come to Chicago to cover the fair and stayed to write "an indictment of Chicago"—*If Christ Came to Chicago*. Jane Addams recalled his visits to Hull-House, "some of them between eleven and twelve o'clock at night, when he would come in wet and hungry from an investigation of the levee district, and while he was drinking hot chocolate before an open fire, would relate one of his curious monologues." Stead made a strong plea for civic reform at a mass meeting in November 1893. His speech hit hard at the unnecessary industrial crisis, which, he maintained, was "due to the lack, the irregularity [of employment], the low pay and excessive hours of work." The "disreputable" classes in Chicago, he insisted, were not the unemployed, but the "rich cultured" men and women who were "dowered with endless opportunity for serving the city" yet "did nothing for its welfare."

Stead's appeal and the deepening economic distress in Chicago led to the organization of the Civic Federation, made up of a group of prominent Chicago businessmen, along with a number of reformers, including Jane Addams. They formed an emergency relief association, and Jane Addams served on the committee to assist the physical needs of the unemployed. Relief stations opened in various parts of the city and temporary lodging houses were established. Money given for this relief was spent "upon the condition that able-bodied men receiving food and lodging shall render an equivalent . . . in labor." Street sweeping was organized to give work to the unemployed men. In 1910 Jane Addams recalled her experiences of the winter of 1893-94: "I resigned from the street cleaning committee in despair of making the rest of the committee understand that, as our real object was not street cleaning but the help of the unemployed . . . it was better to have the men work half a day for seventy-five cents than a whole day for a dollar, better that they should earn three dollars in two days than in three days." The discussions concerning relief drove her to the "most serious economic reading I have ever done." Living in the center of an urban slum that winter was a searing experience. It took all her courage in those hard times to keep up her spirits. "Our neighbors are so forlorn and literally flock to the house for work," she wrote to Mary Roset Smith.

It was during that winter of 1893-94 that Jane Addams, as she said, "became permanently impressed with the kindness of the poor to each other." For the poor, charity was simple and democratic; it was bounded "only by the needs of the recipient and the resources of the giver." Addams developed a full critique of urban charities by observing her neighbors during the winter of 1893-94. Traditional American virtues of hard work and thrift, which the middle class preached to the poor as they doled out their measured charity, were meaningless to families who could find no work, or who needed every cent merely to live. At a symposium entitled "What Shall We Do for Our Unemployed" she urged that the unemployed needed to be consulted.

> They are men; they have practical ideas; they would be glad to do their share to remove this trouble of which they are the chief victims. We ought to come together and regard it as a common trouble, and we should consider not what we shall do with the unemployed, but what we and the unemployed do together that we may all as brothers grow out into a wider and better citizenship than we have ever had.

For Jane Addams, the emancipation of the worker was the central question of industrial America, just as the emancipation of the slave had been the central question of her father's generation. For her, the political institutions of the time were inadequate in creating the kind of social equality that she regarded as central to American democracy. Traditional individualism and self-reliance could not alone solve the problems of America's urban-industrial society. Every social and political institution needed radical change if immigrants and workers were to participate in the decision-making process and if all were to benefit from the American industrial economy. "We have learned to say that the good must be extended to all of society before it can be held secure by one person or any one class," Addams wrote, "but we have not yet learned to add the statement that unless all men and classes contribute to the good, we cannot even be sure it is worth having."

For Jane Addams, the Pullman strike of 1894 was an industrial tragedy that symbolized the clinging to traditional individualism and ignoring "the demands for a more democratic administration of industry." As the fair ended and the depression deepened, unrest developed in the town of Pullman, just twelve miles south of Chicago. Pullman, named after its founder George Pullman, was the center of the railroad sleeping-car manufacturer's enterprises, and in the eyes of its founder, a "model town" for his employees.

George Pullman was one of the most successful industrialists of his age. One of ten children of a general mechanic from upstate New York, Pullman quit school early and worked as a cabinetmaker and a street contractor before coming to Chicago in the 1850's. In 1867 he began mass production of Pullman railroad cars. The bulk of the Pullman Palace Car Company's work was concentrated in an area south of Chicago where, in good times, some five thousand workers repaired and manufactured both Pullman sleeping and parlor cars.

It was there that Pullman realized his vision and constructed after 1880 a 600-acre town with eighteen hundred tenements for his workers. Besides housing, Pullman provided his workers with water, gas, and public buildings, such as a theatre, church, and library containing eight thousand volumes. With many aesthetic and sanitary features such as pretty parks, landscaped lawns, paved streets lined with trees, and regular garbage collection, the town of Pullman was, in the words of its official historian, a community "from which all that is ugly, discordant and demoralized is eliminated."

The town, however, did not in all ways live up to this glowing description. As one of its ministers reported, "The whole impression of the town outside its central part is that it is crowded and unwholesome. The houses are all built in solid brick rows. The monotony and regularity of the buildings give one the impression that he is living in a soldier's barracks."

The presence of the corporation was felt everywhere. As one employee complained, "We are born in a Pullman house, fed from a Pullman shop, taught in the Pullman school, catechized in the Pullman church, and when we die we will be buried in the Pullman cemetery and go to Pullman hell." The Pullman Company owned everything in the town—the land, the plant, the tenements, the library, the theater, the schools, and the church—and kept close control over it all. As employer, George Pullman determined wages. As landlord, he fixed rents and provided gas and water that he got from Chicago and sold at a profit in Pullman.

Trouble began in 1894 when the company ordered wage cuts, while rents and prices remained as high as they had been before. Caught in the squeeze between falling income and fixed prices, many workers were forced to the edge of destitution.

On May 9, 1894, a workers' committee discussed labor's plight with George Pullman and Thomas H. Wickes, a vice-president. The committee demanded restoration of the old pay scale during the first half of 1893. George Pullman refused: The company, he said, was still losing money in spite of the wage cuts. Wickes assured the workers that no action would be taken against them for asking for redress of their grievances.

On May 10, two committee members were laid off, and Pullman workers went out on strike. In June they appealed to the American Railway Union (ARU) for support. They charged that, despite the company's promise, two of their brothers had been fired in retaliation the day after the meeting: This, they said, was the reason for the May 11 walkout.

The American Railway Union was, for the Pullman workers, a voice of hope. Between March and the beginning of the strike, some four thousand Pullman employees enrolled in this union, which had been started the previous spring, led by Eugene V. Debs. Debs had long been involved in various trade unions of railroad skilled workers, called Brotherhoods. He had, however, become disgusted with the warfare of the Brotherhoods, each of which would readily sacrifice another Brotherhood for a selfish gain for its own union. In 1892 Debs resigned from his position in the Brotherhoods stating, "It has been my life's desire to unify railroad employees and to eliminate the aristocracy of labor, which unfortunately exists, and organize them so all will be on an equality."

The American Railway Union, founded a year later, had remarkable success in its first year and grew rapidly. In June 1894 representatives from four hundred sixty-five local units of the union met for their first convention in Chicago. The Pullman workers appealed to these delegates. "We struck at Pullman," they said:

> because we were without hope. We joined the American Railway Union because it gave us a glimmer of hope. . . . We will make you proud of us, brothers, if you will give us the hand we need. Help us make our country better and more wholesome.

The delegates were deeply moved. Debs, however, was cautious about committing his fledgling union to a general railroad strike during the depth of a depression. He suggested further negotiation, but the Pullman Company said there was nothing to arbitrate—wages and working conditions could be determined by company management alone. After a fruitless attempt at negotiation, the convention voted on June 22 "that unless the Pullman Palace Car Company does adjust the grievance before 12 o'clock Tuesday, June 26, the members of the American Railway Union shall refuse to handle Pullman cars and equipment after that date." The boycott thus began at noon on June 26.

Twenty-four railroad companies operating out of Chicago were members of the General Managers Association, which represented their common interests. This group welcomed a chance to break Debs' union, the ARU. The boycott, the railroads declared, was "unjustified." They would fight it "in the interest of their existing contracts and for the benefit of the traveling public."

The railroads then began to fire ARU workers who refused to handle Pullman cars and equipment. Many other railroad workers went out on strike in sympathy. Much of the nation's railroad system came to a standstill.

Jane Addams was one among several individuals and groups who attempted to mediate between the workers and Pullman. As a member of a Citizens Arbitration Committee of the Civic Federation, Addams met with Pullman workers in late May and discovered some of the causes of their discontent. The attempts of the Civic Federation to arbitrate met with no success, as Addams's testimony revealed before the U.S. government commission investigating the strike. "We considered the effort a failure," she said, adding that the officials of the Pullman Company "were always very courteous to me, but they insisted that there was nothing to arbitrate."

The strike was fought out between the railroad companies and the workers to a violent conclusion. Since the railroad managers refused to uncouple a single Pullman car, no passengers or freight could move, and not even a mail car. As the strike spread across the country telegrams arrived Washington reporting that where it was effective the mail service was being paralyzed. In other places, where the companies had been able to hire strikebreakers, violence broke out when hungry and jobless crowds blocked the movement of the cars. In this situation the federal government intervened.

U.S. Attorney General Richard Olney, a former corporation lawyer and director on many railroad boards, believed that a national railway strike was illegal. He advised federal attorneys to initiate legal action against all persons who, by their action, obstructed the passage of regular trains carrying U.S. mail. On July 2 the federal district attorney of Illinois obtained a judicial order, called an injunction, to stop the boycott. A U.S. marshall read this order at Blue Island, a railroad junction south of Chicago, where railroad cars had been overturned, temporarily preventing the passage of any trains. The U.S. marshall then informed Olney that the "rioters" would not obey and that "no force less than the regular troops of the United States can procure the passage of mail trains or enforce the orders of the Court." Olney then persuaded President Cleveland to order federal troops into Chicago, despite the protests of Mayor John P. Hopkins and

Governor Altgeld that city police and state militia were in control.

On July 10 Debs was arrested for conspiracy and contempt of the court injunction that restrained strike leaders from any deed to encourage the boycott. Realizing that if the union leaders obeyed the injunction, the boycott would collapse, Debs decided to ignore it. He declared bitterly that, "the crime of the American Railway Union was the practical exhibition of sympathy for the Pullman employees." The arrest of Debs, not the intervention of federal troops, effectively ended the strike. The presence of federal troops, far from ending the trouble, only heightened the bitterness of the Chicago working class and caused more violence.

After her attempt at conciliation failed, Jane Addams played no further role in the strike, although Hull-House was still very much involved. Florence Kelley was busy trying to raise funds for Debs' defense after he was jailed for ignoring the court injunction.

Jane Addams was away from Chicago much of the time during this period. Her sister Mary died that July after a long illness, and Jane was preoccupied with the family tragedy. When she returned to Chicago after Mary's death, federal troops were encamped around the post office. The city was divided by class hatred. "Each morning during the long weeks of the strike," she wrote, "thousands of children at the more comfortable breakfast tables learned to regard labor unions as the inciters of riot and the instruments of evil; thousands of children at the less comfortable breakfast tables shared the impotent rage of their parents that law is always on the side of capital. . . ."

Jane Addams had great sympathy for the workers and defended their right to organize. With its emphasis on brotherhood, the labor movement seemed to her to be groping toward a social morality that she felt the industrial age demanded. The class hatred generated by a long and bitter strike distressed her. With her vision of human solidarity gained by the experience of living in an immigrant community, Addams rejected the concept of a class society.

Against this she constantly emphasized the importance of a new social morality—"the identification with the common lot which is the essential idea of democracy."

Jane Addams was particularly upset by the cruelty and waste of the Pullman strike as she saw its impact upon her neighbors. Pullman reopened his plant late in the summer of 1894 after he had fired 25 percent of his workers and compelled the rest to sign "yellow dog" contracts pledging that they would never join a union. Addams was familiar, too, with blacklisted workers whose lives had been ruined by the strike.

Addams's reaction to the strike reveals her pacifism. She found it impossible to accept violence as a way of resolving differences between people.

After the strike, she and other members of the Civic Federation successfully agitated for legislation to create a State Board of Conciliation and Arbitration which, she hoped, would mediate labor disputes. The law "embodied the best provisions of the then existing laws for the arbitration of industrial disputes."

For Addams, the Pullman strike was "a drama which epitomized and at the same time challenged the code of social ethics." As much as it was a class conflict, Addams also saw it as a conflict between an outdated, individualistic ethic that included the benevolent impulses of an employer and a social ethic that was the essence of democracy. Addams noted "the manifestation of moral power" in the efforts of the American Railway Union to aid the strikers at Pullman. Here were workingmen groping for a larger social morality in which "the injury of one was the concern of all."

On the other hand, George Pullman was not a bad employer. "The sense of duty held by the president of the Pullman Company," she wrote:

> doubtless represents the ideal in the minds of the best of the present employers as to their obligations towards their employees, but he projected this ideal more magnificently than the others. He alone gave his men so model a town, such perfect surroundings.

Pullman's failure was the failure of the ideal of benevolence. "The president of the Pullman Company," Jane Addams wrote, "doubtless began to build his town from an honest desire to give his employees the best surroundings." But, she said, he became so obsessed with his role as a benefactor, that he lost the power of achieving "a simple human relationship with his employees, that of frank equality." He was, further, totally unable to recognize the nobility of the American Railway Union. Compared with the workingman's ethic— brotherhood and the commitment of each to the cause of all—Pullman's paternalistic ideas of clean living, thrift, and temperance were "negative and inadequate."

Pullman, she concluded, had done much harm. He does not understand, she said, that "the social passion of the age is directed toward the emancipation of the wage-worker. . . ."

Although Jane Addams never came to the defense of striking workers in as direct a fashion as did some of her associates at Hull-House, she did organize relief funds to aid strikers and their families. She also spoke out in behalf of workers in a number of the major Chicago strikes. She advocated conciliation and arbitration, at times personally intervening to present strikers' demands and to explain her stand in support of workers. In many cases she knew both the labor leaders and the leading businessmen involved in a strike, such as the businessmen Joseph Schaffner and Harry Hart in the textile strike of 1910. In that strike she played an important role in bringing the two sides together.

Jane Addams also continued to educate the American public about the aims of the labor movement. In 1899 she published an article on "Trade Unionism and Public Duty," which further developed her view on the role of unions. "Probably the labor-unions come nearer to expressing moral striving in politics than any other portion of the community," she wrote, "for their political efforts in most instances have been stimulated by a desire to secure some degree of improvement in the material conditions of working people."

But it was impossible for trade unions alone to accomplish peaceably what needed to be done for laborers without the support of the public and the intervention of the state. "The public shirks its duty, and then . . . blames the union men for any disaster which arises," wrote Addams. Much of the energy of Hull-House was directed to the awakening of the public and the state to its duty to working men and women in an industrial society.

8

EXCURSIONS INTO POLITICS

During her years at Hull-House, Jane Addams became an expert practical reformer who knew how to marshall evidence and to mobilize support for legislative change. She usually avoided getting directly involved in partisan politics. In 1895, however, she, entered directly into Chicago ward politics and, in attempting to defeat the political boss of the Nineteenth Ward, learned about the operation of party politics at its grass roots.

Jane Addams's challenge to one of the most powerful Chicago ward politicians arose out of her attempts to improve the conditions of her neighborhood. The death rate in the Nineteenth Ward was one of the highest in the city, and its filthy streets and alleys were an obvious source of disease. One of Jane Addams's early efforts was to do something about garbage collection. In 1895 she secured an appointment as garbage inspector for the Nineteenth Ward and rose each morning at six to follow the collection wagons on their rounds. This action brought Hull-House to the attention of ward boss Johnny Powers, who resented the interference of the Hull-House women. He considered the position of garbage inspector as a patronage job.

Johnny Powers was the prototype of the political boss who was becoming an increasingly important figure in American city politics. This short, stocky Irishman, who had been a grocery clerk, ran for alderman of the city council from the Nineteenth Ward in 1888 and became one of the most powerful men in Chicago. As chairman of the city council's Finance Committee and boss of the Cook County Democratic Party, he used his power unscrupulously. He was largely responsible for giving away millions of dollars worth of city franchises to street railway and gas companies. The companies repaid this generous gift fairly cheaply by providing money to Powers, which he used to keep voters loyal to him at election time. In addition, no alderman succeeded so well in getting people from his own ward onto the city payroll. At the same time the streets of the Nineteenth Ward were ill-paved and filthy, and the public school was overcrowded.

The campaign against Powers began modestly, organized by the Hull-House Men's Club, which in 1895, with Addams's encouragement, promoted the candidacy of one of its members as an independent candidate for the second alderman position. In 1896 the campaign against Powers began in earnest as Hull-House tried to unseat Powers himself. Jane Addams played a major role in this effort. Hull-House residents blanketed the ward with posters denouncing Powers's corruption and passed out leaflets detailing the disastrous effects of his power. Powers won the election, but not with his usual margin of victory, which encouraged the residents of the settlement as they prepared to do battle again in 1898.

Jane Addams learned from her experience in the campaign of 1896, and she began the campaign of 1898 with a speech analyzing the source of Powers's power.

There was nothing the immigrants admired so much as simple goodness, Jane Addams said. "The successful candidate must be a good man according to the standard of his constituents." The poor of the Nineteenth Ward were accustomed to helping each other out in times of trouble. It seemed then "entirely fitting that [their] Alderman should do the same thing on a larger scale—that he should help a constituent out of trouble just because he is in trouble." A political boss, like Powers, performed just such a function for his constituents. When a resident of the ward got in trouble with the law, Powers was always there to bail him out. He paid the rent when there was no money and provided work for the unemployed. At Christmas he "distributed six tons of turkeys" and was a friend in times of family need. When death occurred, he provided the appropriate funeral, saving the very poorest from the "awful horror of burial by the county."

It would be difficult for the reformers to discredit Powers with their emphasis on the honesty of government administration. He isn't elected because he is dishonest, Addams stated. "The Alderman is really elected because he is a good friend and neighbor." Although Jane Addams did not approve of Powers's political ethics, she recognized that people were willing to put up with political corruption rather "than give up the consciousness that they have a big, warmhearted friend . . . who will stand by them in an emergency."

Despite the almost insuperable task, Hull-House residents again were ready in 1898 to pit their influence against that of Powers. Led by Hull-House, the civic reformers selected a candidate and organized and financed his campaign. Woman's clubs, Italian clubs, Irish clubs, and Jewish clubs were formed, and each precinct of the ward was organized by the Hull-House Men's Club. Hull-House became a campaign headquarters with residents compiling registration lists and sending out campaign literature.

Johnny Powers fought back with the full force of his power. He tried unsuccessfully to redistrict the Nineteenth Ward in order to cut off the Italian section, which he felt was most seriously under Hull-House influence. He attempted to stir up the Catholic clergy against Hull-House. He spent money freely and used coercion; the small peddlers, for example, who depended on a license from the city to carry on their trade, had their instructions to vote for Powers. When election day came, Powers's assets paid off. As the count began to come in, Jane Addams wrote, despondently, that everything was "as bad as bad can be."

Jane Addams was too practical to waste further effort on Powers, whom she judged impossible to defeat. But the battle between Jane Addams and the ward boss was significant in that it was one of a number of similar battles that would be fought in cities all over the country in the early twentieth century as urban reformers gained support for civic reform. Few of these reformers had quite the viewpoint that Addams had. Since Addams lived with immigrants in the Nineteenth Ward, she knew that urban reform was not just to clean up city hall, but to make city officials respond to the real needs of the people, such as employment, a healthy home, and good schools.

It was a long but not illogical jump from the campaign against Powers in the 1890's to Jane Addams's participation in the Progressive Party campaign of 1912. During the intervening years at Hull-House, a succession of struggles for reform made politics central to the work of Jane Addams and her associates. This work and the national attention it received brought Jane Addams into a position of leadership in the widespread reform movement that was emerging in the United States at the beginning of the twentieth century. Addams now began to devote much of her time to publicizing reforms that had been launched by Hull-House and its residents. Increasingly her days were filled with meetings, speaking tours, and writing.

This was exactly as it should be. Social change cannot be won unless people in large numbers become convinced and are prepared to support such change. Reformers must undertake a struggle that may last for years, generating conflict and debate. In time, if the agitation is successful, the climate of public opinion changes.

Once the climate of opinion is created, it is then possible to frame and enact legislation to accomplish proposed reforms. Jane Addams's influence was thus first felt in the effort to build a climate of opinion to support reform. She began accepting speaking engagements around Chicago early in the 1890's explaining the meaning of settlements in order to raise money for Hull-House. She spoke on many topics, including child labor, the education of immigrants' children, and the labor movement. By 1894 she was accepting engagements from Boston to San Francisco at colleges, woman's clubs, and conferences. In the days before radio and television, many Americans not only went to speeches and lectures as a form of entertainment, but they also received much of their information through such events. Jane Addams was an effective speaker who thought quickly on her feet. She made real the problems she presented.

Addams soon began to rework her speeches and lectures into articles and then used these articles for the books she wrote, the first, *Democracy and Social Ethics*, published in 1902. Through her writing she reached an even wider audience. Although sharply critical of American society, Addams never fundamentally challenged the structure of the American economy. She was optimistic that necessary readjustments could be made without destroying the system. If people only understood their new industrial urban society, she felt they could adapt American democracy to the new circumstances. Hers was a hopeful message, and many of her books became best sellers.

In addition to her role as a publicist of reform, Jane Addams helped organize and served on many committees and organizations, such as the National Federation of Settlements; the National Child Labor Committee, which promoted both state and national legislation against child labor; and the National Association for the Advancement of Colored People, which fought against discrimination against blacks and for the full recognition of their civil rights. Through a vast network of friends, fellow reformers, and Hull-House residents, Addams was connected to almost every grass-roots organization seeking social change in the earlier part of the twentieth century. Few reform efforts that sought to extend social justice in the Progressive era did not have at least one Hull-House alumna or resident among its leaders.

Addams's participation in many of these organizations and her abilities as a skillful administrator and mediator were recognized in 1909 when she became the first woman president of the National Conference of Charities and Correction. The conference was dominated by reform-minded social workers and acted in many ways as an umbrella organization for many of the other organizations on which Addams served. In 1909 the conference appointed a Committee of Industrial Standards to serve as a focus for the concerns of many separately conducted reform agitations. In 1912, an election year, the committee completed a minimum platform to help "direct public thought and secure official action." This platform became the basis of the social and industrial planks of the National Progressive Party.

Jane Addams entered national politics in 1912 because the Progressive Party seemed to consolidate all the reform efforts for which she had been working through many separate organizations for over a decade. Members of the voluntary organizations promoting various reforms had all experienced, as she put it, "the frustration and disappointment of detached and partial effort." "More and more, social workers," she wrote:

> with thousands of other people, had increasingly felt the need for a new party which should represent "the action and passion of the times," which should make social reform a political issue of national dimensions . . . to test its validity by the "inner consent" of their fellow citizens.

Jane Addams also entered national politics because she believed women needed the vote and that the time was ripe to present the issue of equal suffrage to the electorate.

Addams had begun to direct her energies to the issue of woman suffrage in 1907. Although from her college days she had been concerned with the rights of women and their role in society, she had not taken an active role in the suffrage movement. Addams had long advocated that women should have the vote, but as the new century advanced she began actively to work for women's political participation as a necessary instrument to achieve social democracy. She joined the National American Woman Suffrage Association, becoming a vice-president in 1911. In 1907 she campaigned unsuccessfully for municipal suffrage in Chicago and helped to manage an aggressive campaign at the state level for woman suffrage in all elections in Illinois, a victory that came only in 1913. She also argued for women's right and responsibility to take a more active role in government.

Her approach to woman suffrage was quite different from that of the early suffragists, like Elizabeth Cady Stanton who had focused upon the idea of natural rights in the Declaration of Independence. Addams rejected the argument of natural rights as "too barren and chilly" to convince men of the twentieth century. She placed woman suffrage in the history of the evolution of democratic self-government. For Addams, the history of self-government was "merely a record of human interests which had become the subject of government action, and of the incorporation into government itself of the classes who represented the new interests." Since many of woman's traditional concerns, such as the family's health and the safety of her home, were now the business of city health and housing departments, if women "took no part in them now . . . they [would be] losing what they have always had."

In a modern urban society, Addams maintained, women could not even preserve their homes without extending their responsibility. Women in the country, she pointed out, could keep their own doorways clean and "feed the refuse of the table to a flock of chickens." "In a crowded city quarter," Addams wrote:

> if the street is not cleaned by the city authorities no amount of private sweeping will keep the tenement free from grime; if the garbage is not properly collected and destroyed a tenement house mother may see her children sicken and die of diseases from which she alone is powerless to shield them although her tenderness and devotion are unbounded.

While many supporters of woman suffrage were reluctant to extend the vote to working and immigrant women, Jane Addams argued that these women particularly needed it to protect themselves and their families. "The sanitary conditions," she wrote, "of all the factories and workshops, for

Jane Addams campaigns for woman suffrage, speaking from a train platform in 1911

instance, in which the industrial processes are at present carried on in great cities ultimately affect the health and lives of thousands of workingwomen . . . [who] find themselves surrounded by conditions over which they have no control."

Women not only needed the vote to protect themselves and perform their domestic roles properly, but communities also needed the political participation of women. With equal suffrage, women's domestic skill would be reflected in a better urban and industrial environment. "Women," Jane Adams said, "do not wish to do the work of men nor take over men's affairs. They simply want . . . to take care of those affairs which naturally and historically belong to women, but which are constantly being overlooked and slighted by our political institutions." She was convinced that if males were permitted to monopolize government, this would mean that American cities would "continue to lag behind in those things which make a city healthful and beautiful."

Jane Addams challenged neither men's domination of American society, nor the prevailing view of women's separate domestic role. From the perspective of feminists today, her views on women's rights were neither radical nor, in the long run, helpful. Yet her own life was a contradiction of this position. By her example she invited women to change their role and to bring their power and intelligence directly to bear upon the solution of public problems.

Jane Addams's entrance into the Progressive political campaign of 1912 was a pointed challenge to the traditional view of woman's "proper sphere." She faced criticism that by descending into the world of politics she had sacrificed her "superior nonpartisan position." In an article she wrote justifying her action, she revealed both the irony of her position and her own ambition. Women, she pointed out, were praised for undertaking philanthropic work. But when a program became government-run—something Addams always urged—women's "further activity was unwomanly [because] the institution had entered the political field." Welfare services that were begun by women might become a part of government. The services then might be allowed to languish and fail for the absurd reason that women were barred from any further participation or role.

At the Progressive political convention in 1912, all the social concerns to which Addams had given her energies for more than two decades were translated into a national political program—one which she and her friends helped to draft. "Among the members of the Platform Committee for the new Progressive party," she wrote, "were the social workers who had approved three successive reports at the National Conference conventions. . . . One sub-committee would seem to me like a session of the National Conference of Charities and Corrections; another, like a session of the American Sociological Society." Jane Addams was treated as one of the elder statesmen of the convention, given a prominent role not only in the platform committee, but also in the nomination process.

Despite her overall enthusiasm for the party program, Jane Addams recognized important differences between herself and the candidate whose nomination she had seconded. Theodore Roosevelt had taken firm positions at the convention with which she was not in sympathy. She confessed that it had indeed been difficult for her to "swallow" the platform demand for two new battleships a year and a plank endorsing the fortification of the Panama Canal. How could a party pledged to spend money to protect canal workers against yellow fever and malaria and to protect industrial workers against long hours and accidents, threaten with destruction "the same sort of human stuff which it had so painstakingly kept alive."

Another issue more difficult to deal with was Roosevelt's decision not to seat Negro delegates from the Southern states. If Roosevelt was to stand any chance of winning, he would need Southern support, which, in 1912, meant white and often racist support. He made the decision to seat only white delegates from the Deep South.

Jane Addams spoke out against Roosevelt's policy at the convention, along with several other people who were also members of the National Association for the Advancement of Colored People. She pointed out "the inconsistency of pledging relief to the overburdened working man while leaving the colored man to struggle unaided with his difficult situation, if, indeed the action of the credentials committee had not given him a setback."

Despite her reservations about some of Roosevelt's positions, Jane Addams campaigned actively for the Progressive Party, traveling more than 7,500 miles during October and the first week of November to address Progressive rallies. She campaigned not so much to elect Roosevelt as to publicize the political program embodied in the Progressive platform. A political campaign, she wrote in October 1912, was "but an intensified method of propaganda." "During the present campaign," she wrote:

> measures of social amelioration will be discussed up and down the land, as only party politics are discussed, in the remotest farm-house to which the rural free delivery brings the weekly newspaper. . . . The discussion of the Progressive party

platform will surprise many a voter into the consciousness that the industrial situation in America has developed by leaps and bounds without any of the restraining legislation which has been carefully placed about [it] in Europe.

Jane Addams's experience in the campaign only renewed her convictions "that if the community as a whole were better informed as to the ethical implications of industrial wrongs, whole areas of life could be saved from becoming brutalized or from sinking into hard indifference." Despite Roosevelt's popularity and the enormous positive response to Addams's campaign efforts, the Progressive Party lost; Woodrow Wilson became president. "I had expected from the beginning that Mr. Wilson was to be the next President," she told a newspaper reporter. But, she added, "The principles enunciated in the Progressive Platform afforded the opportunity for giving wide publicity to the need for social and industrial reforms." And for Addams that meant those reforms could no

Jane Addams as she looked at the time of the Progressive Party campaign in 1912.

longer be ignored. The Progressive campaign was the high point of Jane Addams's optimism for reform.

In February 1913 she left Chicago for a vacation in Europe and attended an international woman suffrage meeting in Budapest. Although only a delegate, she was recognized by all those attending as the most eminent woman at the conference. She returned six months later to Hull-House to find the prosperity of 1912 gone and unemployment and hard times returned. Later Edith Abbott, a Hull-House resident, recalled Jane Addams's reaction to this economic crisis. "I don't know what to do and haven't even a law to propose as a remedy." Even her political hopes for Progressive Party influence in Congress faded as it became clear that the new political alignment created in 1912 was disintegrating. After his defeat in the election, Roosevelt and his political friends saw no need to continue the party. Events in the world soon made circumstances very different than they were in 1912. In 1914 the war came and it was to test sorely Jane Addams and her ideals in the Progressive campaign.

9

A PACIFIST FACES WAR

War broke out in Europe in August 1914. Jane Addams learned the news while vacationing with Mary Roset Smith at their house on Frenchman's Bay near Bar Harbor, Maine. The grim reality, she wrote, dawned upon her one beautiful morning "when a huge German liner, to our amazement, suddenly appeared at the bottom of a hill on the Island of Mt. Desert upon which our cottage was built."

The captain of the vessel, which was carrying gold bullion, only heard after leaving New York that Britain had declared war against Germany. He turned at once toward the American shore to avoid being captured. "The huge boat in her incongruous setting," said Addams, "was the first fantastic impression of that strange summer when we were so incredibly required to adjust our minds to a changed world. . . ."

For a number of years the European powers had been lined up against each other by military alliances; they had launched an arms race to build up their armies, navies, and weapons of war. On June 18, 1914, the assassination of Archduke Francis Ferdinand of Austria-Hungary by Serbian student nationalists provided the spark that exploded the world into a war that destroyed millions of human beings. Germany, Austria-

Hungary, and Turkey were pitted against France, Russia, Great Britain and, after a while, Italy.

The war began on August 4, 1914, when German armies invaded Belgium. This, for the Germans, was the first step in a lightning offensive to sweep through Belgium and northern France, to seize Paris, and to make themselves the masters of western Europe. The plan began to fall apart almost as soon as the Germans crossed the Belgian frontier and Belgian civilians and soldiers began to fight back. To terrorize the Belgian people into submission, the Germans burned their villages and shot hundreds of men and women. The resistance only became greater. The following month, September 5 to 10, the French waged their own epic struggle against the invader in the battle of the Marne. The Germans suffered a great defeat and withdrew to prepared lines behind the River Aisne. The war settled down to a long stalemate. By the end of October, the opposing sides (Britain had entered the war on France's side in August) faced each other in trenches that stretched all the way from the North Sea to Switzerland.

World War I was the first major war since the invention of new and awesome weapons of destruction such as the machine gun, poison gas, and long-range heavy artillery. These inventions added a fresh dimension of horror to the battlefield; they spelled swift and impersonal slaughter on a massive scale.

For nearly four years each side strove to end the stalemate by blasting gaps in the enemy's lines and breaking through to the rear with its infantry. Armies fought back and forth over a battle zone where the front line trenches at no point were more than a few hundred yards apart. Armies were sacrificed in the long drawn-out agony of attack and counterattack.

World War I challenged Jane Addams's belief that the twentieth-century world was making progress toward peace. She had developed a pacifist position in the decade before the war. It grew out of her vision of Hull-House as a community of people living together in friendship; it was reinforced by her experiences in the working-class immigrant neighborhoods of Chicago. Addams saw the birth of a peaceful international community in a Polish woman helping her German neighbor, or an Italian worker joining a Jewish worker in a union committed to advancing the interests of all workers.

Her pacifism, too, stemmed from her seeking to bring together people in conflict—such as employers and workers—and encouraging them to understand the issues that divided them.

Jane Addams did not begin to think seriously about man's warlike nature until the Spanish-American War broke out in 1898. Then it hit home to her that the faraway conflict was affecting life in the Hull-House neighborhood. Children playing at war in the streets were "slaying Spaniards."

"Addams linked the children's war play with their need for group approval and the spirit of adventure. But she concluded that war was not, by any means, the only possible outlet for such desires; and that it was, indeed, far from the best.

At a peace congress in Boston in 1904 she suggested a "moral substitute" for war. Peace, for her, was no mere phantom, the mere absence of war. "I do not imagine," she said, "if the human race once discovered the adventure to be found in the nourishing of human life, . . . they would look back with much regret. . . ."

Addams developed her thoughts in *Newer Ideals of Peace*, published in 1907. The idea of "nourishing human life," she wrote, had found expression in efforts to conquer disease, to abolish child labor, to cope with the problems of the aged. The "peaceful" struggle of British, French, and American doctors against tuberculosis, for example, had a strong international aspect, with its "international Congresses, its discoveries and veterans, also its decorations and rewards for bravery."

In the fall of 1914 Jane Addams and other settlement workers were concerned with the impact of the war upon American immigrant communities. In September she joined with Lillian Wald, head of the Henry Street Settlement in New York, in calling a conference at the Henry Street Settlement. The war, and what to do about it, was the topic for discussion.

Peace activists who attended the Henry Street meeting did not believe that neutrality toward the European war meant the same as inactivity. They published an indictment of war and stated their conviction that it threatened the survival of democracy and social reform.

The war, they wrote, numbed the sense of "the preciousness of human life." Where war found "a world of friends and neighbors [it] substituted a world of aliens and enemies." It compelled men and women not to love, but to hate one another. War forced servitude upon young men by obliging them to become soldiers and to engage in mass slaughter of other young men. The European war thrust into the trenches "a million youths with cold and fever and impending death." This happened "at a time when we were challenging Reichstag, Parliament and Congress with the needlessness of infant mortality and child labor."

From 1914 to 1917 sentiment in America was not neutral. Although most Americans did not want to get directly involved in the war, they did sympathize with one side or the other.

Some people agitated directly for entering the war on the side of the British and French Allies. Spearheading this propaganda, which gained in pace and intensity, was a vocal minority headed by a number of influential "war hawks," of whom Theodore Roosevelt was the most prominent. American businessmen, coining large profits from the sale of weapons to the Allies, seconded this effort. Individual members of President Wilson's administration carried on their own campaign in Washington for a rapid military and naval buildup in preparation for eventual entry into the conflict.

To fight against this ominous and growing military spirit, the activists who met at the Henry Street Settlement formed the American Union Against Militarism. Until 1917, when the United States declared war against Germany, the group campaigned against the American arms buildup. Jane Addams worked with this group; but she devoted her principal energies to another activist peace organization launched at the same time—the Women's Peace Party (WPP).

The original impetus for the formation of the WPP came from two European feminists, Rosika Schwimmer and Emmeline Pethick-Lawrence. In September 1914 Schwimmer, a Hungarian journalist and activist in the International Women Suffrage Alliance, arrived in America to present President Wilson with a petition that called for a negotiated peace. The petition contained several hundred thousand signatures of women from thirteen countries.

The following month, October, Emmeline Pethick-Lawrence arrived from England for an American speaking tour. Long an activist in the militant British suffrage movement, Pethick-Lawrence became a passionate pacifist after the outbreak of war. Reaching Chicago in November, she joined Schwimmer at Hull-House. Together they aroused great enthusiasm for the peace cause in the city. They then prevailed upon Jane Addams to call a women's congress in the United States. The congress's aim would be to develop a peace program as the basis for common action among the women of Europe and America.

On January 10, 1915, the conference met in Washington, D.C. Three thousand women crowded into the Willard Hotel to form the Women's Peace Party. In her keynote address, Addams charged that even men convinced that the war was unnecessary were not doing enough to bring it to an end. Women, she said, had a special duty to perform in the struggle for peace. Woman's experience as mother, she believed, gave her a sense of the supreme value of human life that men did not always feel. "Women," she later wrote, "who have brought forth men into the world . . . experience a peculiar revulsion when they see them destroyed, irrespective of the country into which these men may have been born."

Addams also deplored the substitution of military values for social values by a nation at war. Women had come to influence public affairs as states had begun to value the nurture of children and the care of the elderly; but such concerns evaporated in the frenzy of war. "Women have a right," she said, "to protest against the destruction of that larger ideal of the State in which they had won a place . . . and to deprecate a world put back upon the basis of brute force . . . a world in which they cannot play a part."

The women drew up a peace platform that called for a convention of neutral countries to mediate between the warring powers; a league of nations; peace education; and, finally, the vote for women. Addams defended the suffrage plank as "absolutely fundamental to the undertaking." This plank limited the appeal of the WPP basically to women who were in favor of woman suffrage, in spite of the preamble to the platform that welcomed all women "who are in substantial sympathy with the fundamental purpose of our organization."

Once WPP was set up, its leaders attempted to build a federation of national organizations in favor of peace. They knew that the hopes of the women who met in Washington would stand little chance of being realized without such a federation.

Thus it was that a National Emergency Peace Conference met in Chicago in the first week of March 1915. Three hundred men and women from all over the United States attended it, representing many groups—socialists, trade unionists, mutual benefit societies, women's groups, and peace organizations. The meeting resulted in the formation of a National Peace Federation with Addams as its chairperson.

Just as she had done earlier in the cause of Progressive reform, Jane Addams attempted to rally the American public to a minimum program for peace through a network of local associations. But the time was now too short. The tide of events was moving against the peace cause. Increasingly Addams and the peace activists found themselves isolated from the mainstream of public opinion. She herself would be bitterly attacked by ultra-nationalists who feared and rejected the international vision of which she was to become the champion.

While Addams was presiding over the Emergency Peace Conference in Chicago, she received a cablegram inviting members of the WPP to an international congress of women both from neutral countries and those that were at war. The congress would be held at The Hague, Netherlands. Addams was invited to preside over the congress. The invitation came from Dr. Arletta Jacobs, an early woman physician in Holland. Dr. Jacobs was active in the International Women's Suffrage Alliance, which had been forced to cancel its own meeting because of the war.

Although Jane Addams was not confident that such a congress could help bring the war to an end, she was flattered to be asked to lead it. A conference of European and American women, united by a desire for peace, appealed to her; it was an heroic endeavour in such dark days of suspicion and hatred among nations; even the international labor movement's internationalist principles had vanished in the universal war fever.

Jane Addams accepted the invitation and enlisted a group of women to go with her. "Of course," she wrote to Emily Balch, a friend who taught economics at Wellesley College, "the whole undertaking . . . may easily fail—even do harm." Maybe women, she wrote to Lillian Wald, who were willing to risk failure, "may be able to break through that curious hypnotic spell which makes it impossible for any of the nations to consider peace." It was a desperate and, uncharacteristically for Addams, an unrealistic gamble. The Hague Congress was a minority of a minority—feminists who were also pacifists.

On April 13, 1915, the Dutch liner *Noordam* sailed from New York for Rotterdam with forty-two American women delegates. Even before they had embarked Theodore Roosevelt attacked the women's action as "silly and base." It was silly, he said, "because it is absolutely futile"; base because "they dare not stand up against wickedness in the concrete." Roosevelt challenged the women "specifically to denounce Germany's invasion of Belgium, and to demand that in the interests of peace the United States do what it can to put a stop to those wrongs."

For the first eight days the voyage across the Atlantic went smoothly. Each day the women met for classes on various aspects of peace; they prepared resolutions, which they planned to submit to the congress. "It is like a perpetual meeting of the woman's club, or the Federation of Settlements," reported Alice Hamilton, who accompanied Jane Addams.

As soon as the ship entered British waters, it was stopped off the coast of England by naval authorities. For four days they waited, unable to land or receive visitors. However, from newspapers delivered to the ship they learned that the British had closed all traffic in the Channel between England and Holland.

Addams read, too, of sharp attacks upon the women's congress. "We were called 'Peacettes,'" she wrote, "and the enterprise was loaded with ridicule of the sort with which we later became only too familiar."

Finally the *Noordam* was allowed to proceed. The group arrived at The Hague just hours before the conference held its opening session. The Channel closing had also delayed the arrival of a large group of British women; when the conference began, this delegation was still waiting for passage.

Most of the delegates came from Holland, but twelve countries were also represented with forty-three women coming from Germany and Austria-Hungary. None of the women claimed to represent the sentiment of the majority of the women in their country, but among those present was a strong sense of solidarity. "What stands out most strongly among all my impressions of those thrilling and strained days at the Hague," Emily Balch recalled, "is the sense of wonder at the beautiful spirit of the brave, self-controlled women who dared ridicule and every sort of difficulty to express a passionate human sympathy, not inconsistent with patriotism, but transcending it."

According to the rules of the congress, two subjects were forbidden: discussion of the responsibility for the war and the methods of conducting it. Although all the women shared a common desire to end the war, they differed on the means to that end. They managed, however, to arrive at a formulation that satisfied all, resolving "an end to the bloodshed," the beginning of peace negotiations, and an establishment of peace based on the recognition of the right of all people to self-government. Neutral nations were urged "to take immediate steps to create a conference of neutral nations which shall without delay offer continuous mediation . . . invit[ing] suggestions for settlement from each of the belligerent nations and in any case . . . submitting to all of them simultaneously, reasonable proposals as a basis of peace."

Rosika Schwimmer proposed that the Congress send a delegation to neutral and belligerent governments to present the mediation resolution and to learn about their attitudes toward mediation. To Alice Hamilton and Jane Addams, Schwimmer's proposal seemed "hopelessly melodramatic and absurd," but her emotional speech to the congress won its approval. Alice Hamilton felt that Jane Addams would never agree to run around Europe to visit the various heads of state, but, as she reported to Mrs. Bowen, a long time Chicago friend, "as she [Jane Addams] talked to the foreigners she saw that in their eyes it was both dignified and important and she consented."

Jane Addams was about to embark on one of the more unusual of many efforts to halt the war. But before she did, the congress created a permanent committee to call another congress at the end of the war. Jane Addams and Dr. Jacobs, along with Alice Hamilton, set out to present the resolutions of the congress to the governments of Great Britain, Germany, Austria, Hungary, Italy, France, and Belgium. During May and June of 1915 they crossed and recrossed international boundaries of countries at war, meeting with the leaders of the warring nations. The signs of war were everywhere; in Berlin "walls [were] placarded and windows full of appeals for money . . . for blinded soldiers, for relief of the widows of heroes of a certain battle, . . . and . . . long lists of the latest casualties"; in Vienna "people looked starved" and "convalescent soldiers hobbled along the street"; and in France, which had been invaded, bitter resentment engulfed all other feeling. Such scenes must have been painful to Addams and spurred her on to find some way out of this destruction of human life and civilization.

Although the statesmen were courteous, they gave the women little encouragement for their neutral mediation proposal. Yet Jane Addams did not think they were entirely hostile to it. "Everywhere, save from one official in France," she recalled:

> we heard the same opinion expressed by these men . . . ; each one said that his country would be ready to stop the war immediately if some honorable method of securing peace were provided; each one disclaimed responsibility for the continuance of the war; each one predicted European bankruptcy if the war were prolonged, and each one grew pale and distressed as he spoke of the loss of his gallant young countrymen; two of them with ill-concealed emotion referred to the loss of their own sons.

The most heartening response came in Austria during an interview with Prime Minister Sturgkh. As Addams apologized, saying, "It perhaps seems to you very foolish that women should go about in this way," the minister banged his fist on the table and responded, "Foolish? Not at all. These are the first sensible words that have been uttered in this room in ten months."

While Jane Addams and Dr. Jacobs visited the capitols of the belligerent countries, another delegation from the congress, including Emily Balch, talked with leaders of neutral countries to see if they would initiate a neutral conference. Although the women initially received some hopeful signs from Sweden, in the end it became clear that no European neutral country was prepared to take action. Any action would thus depend on the United States.

Jane Addams returned to the United States in July to present the resolutions of the congress to President Wilson and share with him the results of her and her colleagues' visits to the European statesmen. When she arrived in New York on July 5, she was not sure what view Americans held regarding The Hague conference. However, a *New York Times* editorial declared that the true significance of her effort, designed to end the war before democratic nations had triumphed, was that it assisted "not peace, but war."

10

FROM AMERICA'S MOST BELOVED TO MOST DANGEROUS WOMAN

On July 19, 1915, about three thousand people gathered in Carnegie Hall in New York City. They came to hear Jane Addams report upon The Hague conference and the talks with leaders of the European nations. Many Americans were worried about the war in Europe, which was already claiming American lives. Only two months before the Carnegie meeting one hundred twenty-eight Americans, along with hundreds of other passengers, had perished when a German submarine torpedoed and sank the British liner *Lusitania*.

The Carnegie Hall audience realized that incidents like the *Lusitania* might well draw the United States into the war. President Wilson had already warned the German government that if American citizens were among the victims of such sinkings, he would hold Germany "to a strict accountability."

Addams, in her address, pointed to two hopeful signs that an early peace might be negotiated. It was true that the European peoples were united, each behind its own government, in support of the war. But, she said, there was a split between the civilian and the military in the governments.

Some civilians feared a long all-out war; they longed "for some other form of settlement."

Another hopeful sign, she continued, was the opposition of youth to the conflict. The war, she said, appeared to be "an old man's war—the young men who were dying . . . and fighting were not the men who wanted the war [or] who believed in the war."

Almost as an afterthought, she added that the young men on both sides loathed and dreaded bayonet charges. "They give them rum in England and absinthe in France, they all have to give them 'dope' before the bayonet charge is possible."

The following day, Addams's speech made front-page news across the country: TROOPS DRINK-CRAZED, SAYS MISS ADDAMS, screeched the headlines. The main point of her report was lost as the press zeroed in upon this one remark. Addams was presented as charging that all soldiers were cowards who had to be drunk before they would dare to fight.

The first public attack came from the pen of popular novelist and war correspondent, Richard Harding Davis. "Miss Addams," wrote Harding in a letter to the *New York Times*, "strips [the soldier] of honor and courage. She tells his children 'Your father did not die for England or France, or for you; he died because he was drunk. . . .' Against this insult, flung by a complacent and self-satisfied woman, . . . I protest."

Other attacks followed. One newspaper called Jane Addams "a silly, vain, impertinent old maid, who may have done good charity work at Hull House, Chicago, but is now meddling in affairs far beyond her capacity." The most venomous comments came from Theodore Roosevelt. By 1915, Roosevelt had thrown his reform program to the winds and was demanding an immediate U.S. declaration of war on Germany. He regarded pacifists like Addams as his enemies and referred to his former political ally as "one of the shrieking sisterhood," and as "poor bleeding Jane."

Addams was dismayed by such attacks. "I had my first experience," she wrote, "of the determination on the part of the press to make pacifist activity or propaganda so absurd that it would be absolutely without influence. . . . "

Addams pressed forward, nonetheless, with her effort to have the United States take the lead in calling a conference of the neutral nations. Such a conference could help bring the warring powers together to discuss an end to the fighting and the conditions for an enduring peace. It was urgent, she believed, that this effort be made as soon as possible—before hatred and hysteria had been fanned to such an intensity that talk of peace would become impossible. Enthusiasm for continuing the war, she pointed out, was sustained largely by the hatred generated by the war itself.

When the war began President Wilson made clear his wish that the United States remain neutral in order to help mediate or encourage an end to the conflict. Privately he was opposed to a conference of neutral nations; he did not believe that the time was ripe for mediation. However, he agreed to meet several times with representatives of women from The Hague conference. The 'hawks,' in the summer of 1915, were pressing for a rapid American arms buildup, which aroused considerable opposition from liberal Democrats in Congress, as well as from the peace groups. Wilson did not wish, at least for the time being, to sever his political relationship with the peace forces and the liberals.

In the summer of 1915, therefore, Jane Addams, along with Emily Balch and Dr. Jacobs, journeyed to Washington, D.C. and presented The Hague conference resolutions to President Wilson in the White House. In these conversations Wilson was noncommittal with respect to a mediation of the conflict. He could not give a definite answer yet, he said; he wanted to "remain free to act in the best way," and so on.

The women's persistent appeals helped draw Wilson's attention to the possible value of the mediation process. In principle, he told them, The Hague proposals impressed him. He was in favor of them even if, for reasons best known to himself, he had no intention of involving himself immediately in the European dispute. There is little doubt that these proposals provided a source for the peace program that he eventually proclaimed as part of his war aims when the United States later became involved in the conflict.

Frustrated as she was by Wilson's continued inactivity on behalf of peace, Jane Addams learned with interest of Henry Ford's offer to organize and finance a neutral conference of private citizens. Ford met with Addams and other members of WPP in November 1915. To dramatize the venture, Ford announced that he had chartered a "peace ship" that would transport the delegates to Stockholm, where the conference would be held. He boasted that this initiative "would get the boys out of their trenches and back home by Christmas Day."

Addams agreed to take part in this expedition; but her friends had serious doubts about it. Their worst fears were soon realized. The planning for the conference was hasty; serious disagreements among the leaders developed while aboard the "peace ship." Ford himself quit the expedition before the ship arrived in Sweden. The whole project was a fiasco. Henry Ford, the expedition, Jane Addams, and the WPP—all were targets for ridicule in the pro-war press.

Addams did not sail on the "peace ship." She became ill with pneumonia on December 1 and was in a hospital when the expedition sailed from New York City. For a full year, until the end of 1916, Jane Addams remained too ill to carry forward her peace activities with any consistency. During this time the United States moved rapidly toward involvement in the European war.

A central factor at this time was the crisis that faced the German government. Exhaustion and war weariness were growing. Even more ominous was the hunger that resulted from the Allied blockade. The blockade, nearly 100 percent effective, had virtually destroyed the country's foreign trade. This crisis situation prompted German leaders to stake everything on a rapid victory and to play what was called "the last card." That card was the unleashing of unrestricted submarine warfare to destroy the overseas trade, which was the

Allied lifeline, and thus bring about the collapse of the Allied war effort.

The German government was, of course, well aware that unrestricted submarine warfare would almost certainly bring the United States into the war. The Germans gambled that success would come so rapidly that the war would be over before American soldiers arrived in any significant numbers. "The U-boat war," Field Marshall Hindenburg, Germany's supreme commander, told the cabinet, "must begin not later than February 1, 1917." The cabinet, reluctantly, agreed.

A second event, occurring in March 1917, created a crisis for the Allies. It was the Russian Revolution that overthrew the Tsar. It soon became clear that, as much as the new Russian government desired to sustain the war against Germany, the war weariness of the peasants and soldiers was so great that the collapse of the eastern front was only a matter of time. The Russian Revolution meant that Germany would be free to divert hundreds of thousands of troops to the western front for a final victorious offensive against Great Britain and France.

President Wilson reacted swiftly to these new developments. On April 2, 1917, he sent a message to Congress asking for a declaration of war against Germany. War fever now gripped the nation; millions lined up behind the president as the United States went to war. Peace sentiment melted away; antiwar activists were reduced to a tiny minority. Jane Addams found herself in lonely opposition, stubbornly posing difficult questions: Can war lead to the unity of humanity so necessary for a real peace? Can war that fans national hatreds to white heat "make the world safe for democracy?"

In the late spring of 1917, Jane Addams spoke to audiences in the Midwest about the patriotism of a pacifist in wartime. She challenged the idea that war would establish social and political justice. "The spirit of fighting," she said, "burns away all those impulses, certainly toward the enemy, which foster the will to justice." We must hold at all times, she added, even after war has been declared, that "war affords no solution for vexed international problems. . . ."

Her remarks fell upon deaf ears. When she gave her speech in Evanston, Illinois, a judge who had long been a supporter of Hull–House, rose at the end of the talk. "I have always been a friend of Miss Addams," he began, "but . . . ."

Addams gently interrupted him. "The 'but,'" she said, "sounds as if you were going to break with me."

"I am going to break with you," the judge answered. "Anything which casts doubt on the justice of our cause in the present war is very unfortunate. No pacifist measures should be taken until the war is over."

Slowly the realization dawned upon her that nobody was listening. She stopped lecturing about peace. "We became convinced," she said, "that it served no practical purpose, and, worse than that, the immediate result was provocative." She began to suffer from a deep sense of spiritual isolation. "The force of the majority," she remembered, "was so overwhelming that it seemed not only impossible to hold one's own against it, but at moments absolutely un-natural. . . ."

There were for Addams moments of agonizing doubt: "Has the individual," she asked herself, "the right to stand out against millions of his fellow countrymen?" Her ultimate con-viction was shaped and tempered by the crisis created by the war. Man's primary allegiance, she affirmed, "is to his own vision of the truth."

This sense of isolation sapped Addams's energy during and after the war. She needed the support and confidence of the public to sustain the flow of her energies. "Most reformers I have known," wrote Alice Hamilton, "have enjoyed, more or less, the sense of being in advance of their times, of belonging to a persecuted minority. This was never true of Jane Addams."

The conclusion of the war in 1918 did not bring an end to hostility toward pacifists in America. The Russian Revolution of 1917 was seen as a challenge to the established order in many countries. As communists made gains in Germany and eastern Europe, the threat of communism seemed real to Americans, even though the actual number of socialists or

communists in the United States was negligible. Hatred of
Germany, which had sustained the war effort, began to ebb; it
was replaced by a hatred of all persons and groups whom the
press, patriotic organizations, and the government branded as
"radical." This included socialists, anarchists, communists,
reformers of all types, and recent immigrants, particularly
those of Russian background.

This Red Scare, as it came to be called, reached its climax
during 1919 and 1920. With little or no evidence, thousands of
labor activists and foreign-born people were arrested, jailed,
and deported.

The climate of opinion was not one in which Jane Addams
could escape attacks upon her ideas and actions. "Any
proposed change," she wrote "was suspect. . . . To advance
new ideas was to be a radical, or even a bolshevik."

In 1920 Addams spoke out to protest the mass arrest and
deportation of those whom the government, without trial or
proof, branded as disloyal. "Hundreds of poor laboring men
and women," she said in a Chicago speech, "are being thrown
in jails and police stations because of their political beliefs. . . .
And what is it these radicals seek? It is the right of free speech
and free thought, nothing more than guaranteed to them
under the Constitution of the United States." She called for an
end to this oppression, which, she said, "is making of
America another autocracy."

To the press this speech indicated that Jane Addams was a
dangerous radical. The Chicago *Tribune* reported it under the
headline, JANE ADDAMS FAVORS REDS. As for the
American Legion, it charged that Hull-House was "the rally-
ing point of every radical and Communist movement in the
country." A publication of the Honorary Society of the
Reserve Officers Training Corps charged that Addams was
"the most dangerous woman in the country."

Rebuffed by her countrymen, Addams continued to work
quietly on behalf of international peace. After the fighting
ended she organized the Second Women's Congress in
accordance with a resolution that had been passed at the earlier
Hague meeting. The women met in Zurich in neutral

Switzerland in May 1919 as work on the Treaty of Versailles was being concluded in Paris. The American delegation set sail in April amidst much criticism in the press.

There was a feeling of comradeship at the Zurich Congress that Jane Addams found very gratifying. One hundred and fifty women, many of whom had become her friends four years earlier at The Hague, sat down together, she recalled, "not in a pretended goodwill . . . but in genuine friendship and understanding."

It was springtime; Zurich was serene and beautiful. But the immense suffering and waste that the war had inflicted could not be forgotten. Reports of starvation in Europe were terrible, for even though the fighting had ended, the Allied blockade of the Central Powers had not been lifted. The French, British, and American governments felt that continuing the blockade was necessary; it was a weapon of war being used to compel the Germans to submit to the Versailles treaty.

The women passed a resolution that they wired to President Wilson in Paris. They condemned the famine in Europe as "a disgrace to civilization." They urged the peace conference at Versailles to raise the blockade and to make food available for all peoples suffering hunger.

Wilson's response was negative. There was little, he said, that he could do.

While the congress was meeting at Zurich, it received an advance copy of the terms of peace which the Allies sought to impose. The women condemned it as an act of folly, which, they said, "will create all over Europe discords and animosities, which can only lead to future wars." The events of the years to come, between 1919 and 1939, would confirm, tragically enough, the truth of this prediction.

The women formed at Zurich a permanent peace organization, the Women's International League for Peace and Freedom. They elected Jane Addams their president. Addams then went to Paris with a women's delegation and presented the Zurich resolutions to the peacemakers at Versailles. She and Alice Hamilton joined a group of British and American Quakers who were visiting Germany in order to make arrangements for the distribution of food.

Jane Addams was shocked by what she saw. "Incredibly pathetic children," she said, many of whom were seriously ill, all of whom were desperately hungry. Returning to the United States, she set out on a speaking tour to report on famine conditions in Europe and to raise funds to purchase food. When she spoke about the need to raise money to feed German children, audiences heckled her and the press charged her with "pro-Germanism."

As Americans turned their backs on the world in the 1920's, Jane Addams's message of international cooperation to solve the pressing postwar economic and social problems fell on deaf ears. She spent an increasing amount of time abroad working for the Women's International League for Peace and Freedom. Europeans and Asians regarded her with respect. They thought of her as America's foremost woman.

In the United States, the Woman's Peace Party—now the American branch of the International Women's League—continued its work under the leadership of a new generation of women. These were pacifists who understood that peace and social justice must go hand in hand.

11

EPILOGUE

On December 10, 1931, an audience in Oslo, Norway, listened intently as a speaker described one of the recipients of the 1931 award. "She is the foremost woman of her nation," he said. "When the need was greatest she made the American woman's desire for peace an international interest. . . . She clung to her idealism in the difficult period when other demands and interests overshadowed peace."

The occasion was the award ceremony for the Nobel Peace Prize. The woman was Jane Addams who, at age seventy-one, just three and one half years before her death in 1935, received world recognition for her efforts on behalf of peace. She was unable to accept the honor in person, having recently undergone an operation to remove a tumor in her lung.

Addams devoted one-half of her prize money to help the jobless in the Hull-House neighborhood. The Great Depression that hit the United States in 1929 had brought unemployment and much suffering to millions. As one writer described it, "there today stretches a sea of misery more appalling than that which discouraged Miss Addams in the nineties."

Jane Addams (right) and another settlement worker, c. 1932.

Addams's acceptance of the Nobel Prize marked a full circle in the American public's attitude toward her. The Great Depression generated in the early 1930's a new movement for social reform; this changed the climate of opinion in the United States. Under the leadership of Franklin D. Roosevelt, the reform program that the Hull-House women pioneered during the 1890's was continued and broadened. The rise of fascism, too, in Germany, and a new threat to world peace underlined Addams's courage and vision as an antiwar activist.

For many years Jane Addams and her Hull-House associates were part of a movement to change America's views concerning the proper scope of government responsibility. Government, they had taught, must meet the needs and the problems facing millions in an industrialized and urbanized society. Government, they had argued, must provide social insurance against accidents, illness, unemployment, and old age; it must lead the way in insuring for all citizens proper food and housing, and proper care for children. During the 1930's the women's goals appeared to be in the process of becoming realized.

When Addams died in 1935 she left behind an enduring legacy. The Women's International League for Peace and Freedom carried on the work that she had begun. Beyond that she taught the American people whom she loved so well a lesson: In a democracy safeguarding the peace cannot be left to government alone; citizens, too, must exercise daily vigilance and must work to defend peace and to make it real. There can, she taught, be no social justice without enduring peace.

Emily Balch wrote after Jane Addams's death, "I think that her greatness had been veiled by her goodness. Men have a curious tendency to turn those of eminent stature into plastic images." Jane Addams's fame as a settlement-house worker "doing good" has obscured her political and intellectual contribution to America's search for a better social order.

BIBLIOGRAPHY

PRIMARY SOURCES

The Jane Addams Papers, edited by Mary Lynn McCree Bryan, are available on microfilm (82 reels) in libraries, including the New York Public Library. The microfilm edition contains correspondence 1868–1935; files on people and topics in which Addams was interested; Addams's writings from 1877–1935, including college essays, speeches, and published articles; Hull-House Association records; Hull-House Investigations and Publications; newspaper and periodical clippings.

Papers of many of Addams's associates shed light on her various activities. The Henry Demarest Lloyd Papers (Wisconsin Historical Society) include letters between Lloyd and the women at Hull-House. The Florence Kelley Papers (Columbia University) illuminate the relationships between Addams and the other women at Hull-House. There is considerable information on Addams and the peace movement in the Lillian Wald Papers (New York Public Library); the Emily Greene Balch papers; and the files of the Women's International League for Peace and Freedom (the last two collections are in the Swarthmore College Peace Collection). Barbara Sickerman, *Alice Hamilton: A Life in Letters* (Cambridge, Mass.: Harvard University Press, 1984) reproduces a number of letters bearing on Jane Addams and Hull-House.

A fine bibliography of Jane Addams's writings is found in John C. Farrell, *Beloved Lady: A History of Jane Addams' Ideas on Reform and Peace* (Baltimore, Md.: The Johns Hopkins Press, 1967).

A modern edition of Addams's first book, *Democracy and Social Ethics*, ed. Anne Firor Scott, has been published by Harvard University Press (1964). *Twenty Years at Hull House* is available in a New American Library paperback edition. Three editions of her selected writings are available: *Jane Addams: A Centennial Reader*, ed. Emily Cooper Johnson (New York: The Macmillan Company, 1960); *The Social Thought of Jane Addams*, ed. Christopher Lasch (Indianapolis: Bobbs-Merrill, 1965); and *Jane Addams on Peace, War and International Understanding 1899-1932*, ed. Allen F. Davis (New York: Garland Publishing Inc., 1976).

BIOGRAPHY

James Webber Linn, Addams's nephew, wrote the first biography, *Jane Addams, a Biography* (New York: Appleton-Century, 1935). Reprinted many times, Linn's book contains valuable detail of a personal nature. John C. Farrell, *Beloved Lady*, stresses the importance of Addams's thought for her own time, and the relation between her reform ideas and pacifism. Daniel Levine, *Jane Addams and the Liberal Tradition* (Madison: State Historical Society of Wisconsin, 1971), deals with the continuing vitality of Addams's thought in the American reform tradition. Allen F. Davis, *American Heroine: The Life and Legend of Jane Addams* (New York: Oxford University Press, 1973), explores her public image and reputation. This book, perhaps, presents a somewhat distorted view of her personality.

Jill Kathryn Conway, *The First Generation of American Woman Graduates* (New York: Garland Publishing Inc., 1987), deals with Addams and her close associates at Hull-House, also with Lillian Wald. Conway's book shows how each of these educated women defined their roles as women and as professional or public figures in a cultural tradition that made a sharp separation between men's and women's spheres.

Jane Addams was a person whose stature and contribution transcended her own times. The biography that does justice to her as a major figure in American history remains to be written.

THE UNITED STATES 1860-1935

Useful information on the cultural context of Jane Addams's life is provided by the following:

Allen F. Davis, *Spearheads for Reform: The Social Settlements and the Progressive movement, 1890-1914* (New York: Oxford University Press, 1967). An excellent study of the relationship of the settlements and the reform movements of the early twentieth century.

Marie Louise Degan, *The History of the Woman's Peace Party* (Baltimore: The Johns Hopkins Press, 1939). An older but thorough study that has not been superseded.

Ray Ginger, *Altgeld's America* (New York: Funk & Wagnalls Co., 1958). A vividly written account of the times of Jane Addams in Chicago and details of the many reformers with whom she was associated.

Eric F. Goldman, *Rendezvous with Destiny, a History of Modern American Reform* (New York: Alfred A. Knopf, 1952). An enthusiastic and exciting history of American reform movements from the 1870's to the 1940's.

William E. Leuchtenburg, *The Perils of Prosperity, 1914-1932* (Chicago: The University of Chicago Press, 1958). A lively survey of the post World War I years that puts the era into the full context of American history.

C. Roland Marchand, *The American Peace Movement and Social Reform 1898-1918* (Princeton, N.J.: Princeton University Press, 1972). An excellent study of the changes in the peace movement from the prewar organizations to the organizations that emerged with World War I.

George E. Mowry, *Theodore Roosevelt and the Progressive Movement* (Madison: 1946). A standard biography of Roosevelt, emphasizing his reform program.

Bessie Louise Pierce, *History of Chicago: The Rise of a Modern City 1871-1893* (New York: Alfred A. Knopf, 1957). An extensive and reliable history of Chicago, describing the background of the work of the women at Hull-House.

Nancy Woloch, *Women and the American Experience* (New York: Alfred A. Knopf, 1984). A general history of women in America with an extensive bibliography of the large number of monographs that have been produced since the 1960's, many of which are illuminating for the life of Jane Addams.

INDEX

Stevens, Alzina Parsons, 70-71, 73
Strikes, 85; *see also* Pullman strike
Sturgkh (prime minister of Austria), 108
Suffrage movement: British, 103; *see also* Woman suffrage
Suffragists, 10, 93
Sweating system, 8, 46-47, 67, 71-73

Taft, William Howard, 7
Textile industry, 70
Theater, commercial, 54-55
Toynbee, Arnold, 37
Toynbee Hall, London, 10, 37-38, 39, 49
"Trade Unionism and Public Duty" (Addams), 85
"Tramp boys," 53
Treaty of Versailles, 116
Tuberculosis, 22, 101
Twenty Years at Hull-House (Addams), 22
Typhoid fever, 43

Unemployment, 76, 77, 78, 98
Unions, 62, 72, 85-86; railroad, 80-81
U.S. Children's Bureau, 65
U.S. Congress: House Judiciary Committee, 10
University of Zurich, 66
Urban culture, 52, 57, 59-60, 61
Urban-industrial society, 3, 78, 91; government role in, 120; women and, 93-94
Urban reform, 90
Urban youth (Chicago), 51-60

Vassar College, 27, 63

Wald, Lillian, 101
"War hawks," 102
Weber, George, 15

Welfare services, 95
Wellesley, 27
"What Shall We Do for Our Unemployed" (symposium), 78
Wickes, Thomas H., 80
Wilson, Woodrow, 97, 108, 116; and World War I, 102, 103, 109, 111-12, 113
Woman suffrage, 9-10, 12, 13, 92-94, 104; international meetings regarding, 98
Woman's labor movement, 70
Woman's Medical School, Northwestern University, 68
Woman's Rights Convention, Seneca Falls, N.Y., 9-10
Woman's Trade Union League, 8
Women: education of, 27-28, 30, 66; in industry, 71, 72, 73; occupational choices of, 32,33; and the peace program, 103-4; political participation of, 3, 9, 12, 13, 93-94; Progressive Party and, 4, 6; rights of, 92, 95; social and public role for, 11; work of, 19-20; *see also* Working women
Women, educated, 32-33, 35; career options, 32-33; efforts to reconcile career and family, 33-34; influence of fathers on lives of, 23, 63, 65-66, 68; in social work, 36, 39, 69
Women's International League for Peace and Freedom, 116, 117, 120
Women's Medical College of Pennsylvania, 32, 33
Women's Peace Party (WPP), 103-4, 105, 112, 117
Women's role, 30, 92; effect of higher education on,